GREECE IN POETRY

HARRY N. ABRAMS, INC., PUBLISHERS

GREECE IN POETRY

WITH PAINTINGS,
DRAWINGS, PHOTOGRAPHS,
AND OTHER
WORKS OF ART

EDITED BY

SIMONI ZAFIROPOULOS

THIS BOOK IS DEDICATED TO THE MEMORY OF
MY LATE HUSBAND, EDWIN KUH.

GREEK IN HEART AND SPIRIT

Editor: Adele Westbrook

Designer: Carol Ann Robson

Photo Research, Rights and Permissions: J. Susan Sherman

Library of Congress Cataloging-in-Publication Data
Greece in poetry : with paintings, drawings, photographs, and other
    works of art / edited by Simoni Zafiropoulos.
        p.   cm.
    Includes bibliographical references and indexes.
    ISBN 0–8109–3379–9
    1. Greece—Poetry.   2. Greece—Pictorial works.   I. Zafiropoulos,
Simoni.
PN6110.P7G7   1993
881.008'032495—dc20

                                                        92–30001
                                                        CIP

Page 1: DELPHI CHARIOTEER, detail of the head. c. 477 B.C.
Bronze. *Archaeological Museum, Delphi. Photograph: David Finn,
New York*

Pages 2–3: THE DANCING HORAE from the Theater of
Dionysos, Athens.
1st century, B.C.
Bas-relief, marble.
National Archaeological Museum, Athens.
Photograph: TAP Service, Athens

Page 3: ARCHAIC HEAD IV by Roy Lichtenstein. 1988.
Patinated Bronze.
© *Roy Lichtenstein.*
Courtesy Castelli Gallery.
Photograph: © Dorothy Zeidman 1989

CONTENTS

My parents were from Delphi. According to Greek myth, two eagles sent out by the god Zeus met in Delphi, the "navel" of the earth. So, I feel fortunate to have been born in the exact center of the world and to have imbibed the same waters flowing from the stream of Castalia as the priestesses of Apollo (the Pythia), whose utterances at his shrine exercised such a decisive effect upon ancient Greek life.

Today, as I travel throughout the world, it never ceases to surprise me that even in the most remote areas, Greece is perceived more as an idea or ideal than as a modern reality —in a Dogon village in Mali, young children know about the politics of ancient Greece, and in a small village in Rajasthan in India, the chief of the village recalls the stories about Alexander the Great's expedition to India.

Two years ago I was talking to Paul Gottlieb about a book on the affinity of ancient Greek art and modern art. Paul asked me: "What about Greece in poetry? Poetry started in Greece." And that is how the idea for this book took root.

Within these pages you will find a selection of poems and illustrations that are intended to answer the questions: "What is Greece? And what is Greece in poetry?"

When I asked friends in the United States what Greece suggested to them, the answers were diverse: the light, the sea, the rocks, the Greek people—their passion, their music, the combination and dichotomy of Zorbas dancing on the sand and the Delphi Charioteer smiling serenely across the centuries. Greece is all this, plus a mystical element and . . . the struggle.

During the last fifty years, Greece, a small country of ten million people, has produced two great modern poets who have been awarded Nobel Prizes—George Seferis in 1963 and Odysseus Elytis in 1979.

They are the inheritors of a poetic tradition that began over three thousand years ago on the Aegean Islands and along the coast of Ionia, where Homer produced his two heroic epics, the *Iliad* and the *Odyssey*. It is in these two epics that we encounter the beginning of Western literature.

As the well-known scholar Constantine Trypanis has observed: "Poetry written in Greek constitutes the longest uninterrupted tradition in the Western world. . . . It is Greek poetry that has given the world the various poetic genres in which Western man has expressed his emotions and so many of his thoughts to the present day."

Greece, "born" forty centuries ago on the shores of the Aegean Sea and the Peloponnesus, was "reborn" in the middle of the last century when it gained its independence in 1828. Throughout the four hundred years of Turkish occupation, only folk songs expressed in the most authentic way the pulse of Greek life, its hope and pain. The poet Apostolos Melachrinos claims that, "The Greek race survived its hard experience because it has never stopped singing."

The truth of this is obvious in the way Greeks sing their poetry, and how they live with poetry. Most of the well-known works by our poets have been adapted as lyrics for songs, and thus belong to everyone.

Although contemporary poetry has its roots in the Greek past, it is also haunted by the penumbrae of this past. George Seferis expresses the tremendous weight of this accumulated "burden" of tradition in the following lines:

"I woke with this marble head in my hands.
It exhausts my elbows and I don't know where
to put it down . . ."

It is this past that the poet tries to forget, but it is always present; a nostalgia for the "lost glory," the "vanished world," that can never be completely exorcised.

The lure of *Hellas* (Greece) has been celebrated not only by the Greeks, but also by a coterie of philhellenes. Writers and travelers such as Lord Byron, Shelley, and Keats came in search of the "haunted holy ground," and "the glory that was Greece." And even if the words of Goethe: "Every civilized man ought in some way to be Greek . . ." may sound somewhat remote today, the miracle and the magic remain very much alive.

It is this inexplicable magic that Henry Miller felt upon entering the ancient theater of Epidaurus: "I never knew the meaning of peace until I arrived at Epidaurus. There, there was nothing more to conquer. An ocean of peace lays before me . . ."

Greece is also a sense of harmony, the feeling of being "wind for the kite and kite for the wind, even when the sky is missing," as the poet Odysseus Elytis sings.

Greece is the luminous, turbulent, radiant, silvery sea and the rugged coast. It is also grave stelae, wild figs, wooden tables piled high with tomatoes, olives, and fresh goat cheese, whitewashed, sun-drenched walls, evocative chapels with faded frescoes . . .

In modern Greek, *grafo* means "I write," but the original meaning of the word in antiquity was "I paint," so the one hundred poems included in this book are accompanied by illustrations.

The visual image and the spoken word have always been, and remain, closely linked. Ilustration is simply another form of translation that can interpret and reinforce a text with great sensitivity.

In contemporary Greece there is an enduring bond between artists and poets. When George Seferis saw the "Painted Comments" by the artist, Yannis Moralis, that had been prepared for Seferis's "Selected Poems," the poet said: "Coupling Poetry and Painting together seemed always to me like two horses harnessed to the same carriage, but suddenly pulling in opposite directions. When I saw the paintings, I realized that they are two unfettered horses galloping free on a green field."

Moreover, it is not only Greek artists who have been inspired by Greece, ancient or modern—artists such as Marc Chagall, Giorgio de Chirico (born in Greece), Georges Braque, Roy Lichtenstein, and Robert Rauschenberg, among many others, have drawn upon Greek themes, as well.

"Visual feelings" have also found expression in a variety of works of art such as statues, vases, frescoes, Byzantine icons, naive paintings, and photographs of modern life that you will find in tandem with many of the poems selected for this volume.

The dream and vision of this book is to share a panoply of feelings and emotions with the reader—to make it possible for everyone to see the angelic light of Attica, to touch the bare land, to smell the thyme and orange blossoms, to hear the song of the waves. It is not an exhaustive presentation of Greek poetry, nor an academic one, and there has been no attempt to include all modes or trends in poetry. This work emerges fom the heart and the soul of a Greek enchanted by Greece and by Greek poetry.

And, even if I agree with the words of the historian Ion Dragoumis that, "a pot of basil may symbolize the soul of a people better than a drama by Aeschylus," I deeply believe that we need both.

Many people assisted in making this book possible. Those individuals from Harry N. Abrams, Inc., who have given me the opportunity to see my idea in print I especially thank: my publisher and friend, Paul Gottlieb, a passionate Grecophile, for his warm support, vision, and enthusiasm, and his valuable assistant, Toula Ballas, herself a Greek, a friend and encouraging spirit from the beginning of the project. I also want to thank Adele Westbrook, my editor, for her guidance and

unique ability to put in order thirty centuries of history and art in a very limited space and in precious little time. Susan Sherman, my picture editor, also under severe time constraints, energetically provided insightful and sensitive judgment during the photographic treasure hunt, while my designer, Carol Robson, combined images and poetry with perceptive ability and comprehension so that we may see and feel the visible and invisible Greece.

ACKNOWLEDGMENTS

I never imagined that this book would take so much time to complete, nor that I would have the opportunity to meet so many new and interesting people who have made my life richer.

Let me apologize in advance to anyone I have forgotten. Special warm thanks go to everyone mentioned below.

In Greece: Michael Cacoyannis, Anna Engonopoulos, Dionyssis Fotopoulos, Nikos Hatzikyriakos-Ghikas, Melina Mercouri, Yannis Moralis, Yannis Pappas, Lena Savidi, Anna Sikelianos; and Professors George Giatromanolakis, Michalis Kopidakis, and Carolos Mitsakis.

In the United States: Dr. Vartan Gregorian; Princeton University: Professor Edmund Keeley, Dimitris Gontikas, and special thanks to Maria Hatzegeorgiou for her invaluable help in the research for this project; Kenneth Koch, Dorothy Gregory at Columbia University; Stratis Haviaras at Harvard University.

Institutions in Athens: Benaki Museum: Angelos Delivorias, Director, his staff and the Photographic Archive; Byzantine Museum: Myrto Potamianou, Director, and its Curators; Commercial Bank of Greece: Department of Publications; Greek Literary and Historical Archives (ELIA): Manos Haritatos, Director; Greek National Tourist Organization: Pericles Sampanidis, Director of Advertising, Nikos Costopoulos in the Art Department; A.G. Leventis Foundation: Ambassador Archileas Exarchos; National Archaeological Museum: Olga Alexandri, Director, and its Curators; National Bank of Greece: Dimitris Daskalopoulos, Publications; National Gallery and Alexandros Soutzos Museum, Athens: Marina Lambraki-Plaka, Director, and its Curators; Vouros-Eutaxias Museum of the City of Athens: Dimitris Michalopoulos, Director.

And, I want to express my deepest appreciation to Gianna and Takis Mimi, George Zafiropoulos, and Morton Fink for their enthusiastic support and understanding throughout this long voyage.

SIMONI ZAFIROPOULOS

FROM AXION ESTI
Odysseus Elytis (Born 1911)
TRANSLATED BY EDMUND KEELEY AND GEORGE SAVIDIS

FROM THE GENESIS

IN THE BEGINNING the light And the first hour
              when lips still in clay
              try out the things of the world
      Green blood and bulbs golden in the earth
      And the sea, so exquisite in her sleep, spread
      unbleached gauze of sky

My soul called out for a Signalman and Herald
                              I remember seeing then
                              the three Black Women
           raising their arms toward the East
           Their backs gilded, and the cloud they were leaving behind
           slowly fading
                              to the right And plants of other shapes
           It was the sun, its axis in me
           many-rayed, whole, that was calling And
     the One I really was, the One of many centuries ago
     the One still verdant in the midst of fire, the One still tied to heaven
                              I could feel coming to bend
                              over my cradle
     And his voice, like memory become the present,
     assumed the voice of the trees, of the waves:
                              "Your commandment," he said, "is this world
                              and it is written in your entrails
                              Read and strive
                              and fight" he said
     "Each to his own weapons" he said
     And he spread his hands as would
     a young novice God creating pain and mirth together
          First the Seven Axes, wrenched with force,
          pried loose from high up in the battlements,
          fell to the ground
                              as in the great Storm
                              at its zero point
                              where a bird gives forth its fragrance
                              from the beginning again
     the blood was homing clean
     and the monsters were taking on a human shape
                         So very manifest, the Incomprehensible
          Then all the winds of my family arrived too
          the boys with puffed-out cheeks
          and tails green and broad, mermaidlike
                              and others, old men: familiar, ancient
                              shell-skinned, bearded
          And they parted the cloud in two, and these again into four
          and what little remained they blew away, chasing it off to the North
          With broad foot and proudly, the great Tower trod the waters
     The line of the horizon flashed
     so visible, so dense and impenetrable
                              THIS the first hymn.

9

FROM THE ODYSSEY: A MODERN SEQUEL
Nikos Kazantzakis (1883–1957)
TRANSLATED BY KIMON FRIAR

PROLOGUE

O Sun, great Oriental, my proud mind's golden cap,
I love to wear you cocked askew, to play and burst
in song throughout our lives, and so rejoice our hearts.
Good is this earth, it suits us! Like the global grape
it hangs, dear God, in the blue air and sways in the gale,
nibbled by all the birds and spirits of the four winds.
Come, let's start nibbling too and so refresh our minds!
Between two throbbing temples in the mind's great wine vats
I tread on the crisp grapes until the wild must boils
and my mind laughs and steams within the upright day.
Has the earth sprouted wings and sails, has my mind swayed
until black-eyed Necessity got drunk and burst in song?
Above me spreads the raging sky, below me swoops
my belly, a white gull that breasts the cooling waves;
my nostrils fill with salty spray, the billows burst
swiftly against my back, rush on, and I rush after.
Great Sun, who pass on high yet watch all things below,
I see the sun-drenched cap of the great castle wrecker:
let's kick and scuff it round to see where it will take us!
Learn, lads, that Time has cycles and that Fate has wheels
and that the mind of man sits high and twirls them round;
come quick, let's spin the world about and send it tumbling!
O Sun, my quick coquetting eye, my red-haired hound,
sniff out all quarries that I love, give them swift chase,
tell me all that you've seen on earth, all that you've heard,
and I shall pass them through my entrails' secret forge
till slowly, with profound caresses, play and laughter,
stones, water, fire, and earth shall be transformed to spirit,
and the mud-winged and heavy soul, freed of its flesh,
shall like a flame serene ascend and fade in sun. . . .

Drawing of ULYSSES by Nikos Hatzikyriakos-Ghikas
for the book *Odyssey*, by Nikos Kazantzakis. 1939.
Photograph: Courtesy the artist

HELIOS from the Temple of Athena at Troy.
Variously dated in the 3rd and 1st centuries, B.C. Metope.
Staatliche Museen zu Berlin-Antikensammlung.
Bildarchiv Preussischer Kulturbesitz, Berlin

TO THE SUN (FROM THE ORPHIC HYMNS)
Anonymous (c. 7th century B.C.)
TRANSLATED BY APOSTOLOS N. ATHANASSAKIS

Hearken, O blessed one, whose eternal eye sees all,
Titan radiant as gold, Hyperion, celestial light,
self-born, untiring, sweet sight to living
 creatures,
on the right you beget dawn and on the left night.
You temper the seasons as you ride your dancing
 horses,
and rushing swiftly, O fiery and bright-faced
 charioteer,
you press on your course in endless whirl
and, harsh to the impious, you teach good to the
 pious.
Yours the golden lyre and the harmony of cosmic
 motion,
and you command noble deeds and nurture the

Piping lord of the world, a fiery circle of light
is your course, and, O Paian, your light gives life
 and fruit.
Eternal, pure, father of time, O immortal Zeus,
you are the clear, brilliant, and all-encompassing
 cosmic eye,
both when you set and when you shine your lovely
 and radiant light.
A paragon of justice, O water-loving lord of the
 cosmos,
you guard pledges and, ever the highest, you help
 all.
Eye of justice and light of life, O charioteer,
with screaming whip you drive the four-horsed
 chariot on.
Hear my words and show life's sweetness to the
 initiates.

DELPHIC DAWN (FROM ION)
Euripides (480–406 B.C.)
TRANSLATED BY RONALD FREDERICK WILLETTS

Look, now the sun's burning chariot comes
Casting his light on the earth.
Banned by his flame, the stars flee
To the awful darkness of space.
The untrodden peaks of Parnassus,
Kindling to flame, receive for mankind
The disk of the day.

    The smoke of unwatered myrrh drifts
To the top of the temple.
The Delphian priestess sits on the
Sacred tripod chanting to the Greeks
Echoes of Apollo's voice.

    You Delphians, attendants of Phoebus,
Go down to Castalia's silvery eddies:
When you have bathed in its holy dews,
Return to the temple.
Let your lips utter no words
Of ill-omen, may your tongues
Be gracious and gentle to those who
Come to the oracle.

(LINES 82–101)

THE LAND

ALKINOOS' GARDEN (FROM THE ODYSSEY, BOOK VIII)
Homer (? 9th century B.C.)
TRANSLATED BY ROBERT FITZGERALD

To left and right, outside, he saw an orchard
closed by a pale—four spacious acres planted
with trees in bloom or weighted down for picking:
pear trees, pomegranates, brilliant apples,
luscious figs, and olives ripe and dark.
Fruit never failed upon these trees; winter
and summer time they bore, for through the year
the breathing Westwind ripened all in turn—
so one pear came to prime, and then another,
and so with apples, figs, and the vine's fruit
empurpled in the royal vineyard there.
Currants were dried at one end, on a platform
bare to the sun, beyond the vintage arbors
and vats the vintners trod, while near at hand
were new grapes barely formed as the green bloom fell,
or half-ripe clusters, faintly coloring.
After the vines came rows of vegetables
of all the kinds that flourish in every season,
and through the garden plots and orchard ran
channels from one clear fountain, while another
rushed through a pipe under the courtyard entrance
to serve the house and all who came for water.
These were the gifts of heaven to Alkinoos.

(LINES 119–141)

THE SYMPHONY OF SPRING by Nicolaos Ghyzis.
Late 19th century.
Oil on wood.
National Gallery, Alexandros Soutzos Museum, Athens

PSALM AND MOSAIC
FOR A SPRINGTIME IN ATHENS (FROM THE SIBLINGS)

Odysseus Elytis (Born 1911)

TRANSLATED BY NANOS VALAORITIS

Spring violet fragment
Spring down of a dove
Spring multicoloured dust

    On the open books and papers
    A warm little breeze was blowing
    With gypsies it caught up
    Like
    Kites
    In the air
    And birds trying out their new rudders

Spring bitter lentisk
Spring vapour of the armpits
Spring invisible sesame

    Along a wire that flashed with fire
    On a streetcorner with Caryatids
    A tram
    Screeched by
    The sun in the empty terrain scraped with tongs
    The nettles and the snail-marked grass. . . .

GOLD MYRTLE WREATH from Derveni, Macedonia.
330 B.C.
Archaeological Museum of Thessaloniki.
Photograph: Courtesy Greek National Tourist Organization, Athens

A WREATH
Yannis Ritsos (1909–1991)
TRANSLATED BY EDMUND KEELEY

Your face was hidden in the leaves.
I cut the leaves one by one to get near you.
When I cut the last leaf, you were gone. Then
out of the cut leaves I wove a wreath. I didn't have
anyone to give it to. I hung it on my forehead.

DEMETER AND KORE, Thessaly. First quarter of 5th century B.C.
Marble stele. *Musée du Louvre, Paris.*
Photograph: Caisse nationale des monuments historiques, Paris

HELIODORA'S BROWS
Meleager (c. 90 B.C.)

TRANSLATED BY PETER WHIGHAM

Wreathe violets white
myrtle & slight
narcissus wreathe
wreathe laughing lilies
crocus & hyacinth
yellow, blue
Love's friend the rose:

Heliodora's
myrrhed brows,

wreathed curls
swim in petals.

The petals fall from Heliodora's image
that, flower of flowers, outfaces all.

TO DEMETER (FROM THE HOMERIC HYMNS)
Hesiod (c. 800 B.C.)

TRANSLATED BY THELMA SARGENT

(PERSEPHONE)

She with her friends, the full-breasted daughters of Ocean,
Gathered the flowers that grew in the soft, grassy meadow—
Roses and crocuses, beautiful violets, iris,
Hyacinth, too, and a magical, glowing narcissus,
Which, by the will of Zeus and as a boon to lord Hades,
Gaia sent forth as bait for the flowerlike girl.
A marvel to see was this plant for all gods and mortals:
Out of its root grew a hundred miraculous blossoms
Perfumed with headiest sweetness; all of broad heaven above
And the whole earth laughed, and the salt waves of the sea.
The girl, in astonishment, reached out with both eager hands
To take the lovely new toy. But earth of broad highways gaped wide,
And out of the cleft in the Nysan plain, driving
His immortal horses upon her, rushed lord Polydegmon,
Hades, the many-receiving, many-named son of Cronos. . . .

OUR LAND
Yannis Ritsos (1909–1991)

TRANSLATED BY EDMUND KEELEY

We climbed the hill to look over our land:
fields poor and few, stones, olive trees.
Vineyards head toward the sea. Beside the plow
a small fire smoulders. We shaped the old man's clothes
into a scarecrow against the ravens. Our days
are making their way toward a little bread and great sunshine.
Under the poplars a straw hat beams.
The rooster on the fence. The cow in yellow.
How did we manage to put our house and our life in order
with a hand made of stone? Up on the lintel
there's soot from the Easter candles, year by year:
tiny black crosses marked there by the dead
returning from the Resurrection Service. This land is much loved
with patience and dignity. Every night, out of the dry well,
the statues emerge cautiously and climb the trees.

Life on Mount Athos.
c. 1930.
Benaki Museum, Athens. Photographic Archive
Photograph: Nelly's

FROM ODE ON A GRECIAN URN
John Keats (1795–1821)

V

O Attic shape! Fair attitude! with brede
   Of marble men and maidens overwrought,
With forest branches and the trodden weed;
   Thou, silent form, dost tease us out of thought
As doth eternity: Cold Pastoral!
   When old age shall this generation waste,
     Thou shalt remain, in midst of other woe
Than ours, a friend to man, to whom thou say'st,
   "Beauty is truth, truth beauty,"—that is all
     Ye know on earth, and all ye need to know. . . .

PARTHENON AND ALLEGORY OF ENSLAVED GREECE
by Joseph Mallord William Turner.
1822. Watercolor. *Vouros-Eutaxias Museum of the City of Athens*

LUMINOUS LANDSCAPE, NIGHT. Porto Raphti, Greece.
1980.
Photograph: © Daniel Schwartz, Zürich

FROM CLOUDS
Aristophanes (450–385 B.C.)
TRANSLATED BY KENNETH MCLEISH

Rise up and come, immortal Clouds.
In a sparkle of raindrops, rise
From the swollen sea; rise up
To the peaks of the high hills

Shaggy with trees; look down
On the distant view,
Meadows and water-gardens,
Rippling streams, the booming sea.
The sun's unblinking eye
Sparkles with light: shake free
A mantle of rain over all the earth.
Immortal Clouds, rise up and come.

(LINES 275–290)

ATHENS (FROM ODE TO LIBERTY)
Percy Bysshe Shelley (1792–1822)

Athens arose: a city such as vision
    Builds from the purple crags and silver towers
Of battlemented cloud, as in derision
    Of kingliest masonry: the ocean-floors
Pave it; the evening sky pavilions it;
        Its portals are inhabited
        By thunder-zoned winds, each head
Within its cloudy wings with sun-fire garlanded,—
    A divine work! Athens, diviner yet,
        Gleamed with its crest of columns, on the will
    Of man, as on a mount of diamond, set;
        For thou wert, and thine all-creative skill
Peopled, with forms that mock the eternal dead
    In marble immortality, that hill
    Which was thine earliest throne and latest oracle.

Reconstruction of the Parthenon by Benoit Loviot (detail).
1879–81.
Watercolor.
École Nationale Supérieure des Beaux-Arts, Paris

Column fragments at Olympia.
1930s.
Benaki Museum, Athens. Photographic Archive
Photograph: Nelly's

OLYMPIAN X (FROM THE ODES)
Pindar (c. 438 B.C.)
TRANSLATED BY C. M. BOWRA

The strong son of Zeus drove the whole of his host
And all his booty to Pisa,
And measured a holy place
For his mighty Father.
He fenced the Altis and marked it off
In a clean space, and the ground encircling it
He set for rest at supper,
In honour of the Ford of Alpheos

And the twelve Kings of the Gods.
To Kronos' Hill he gave a name; for before
It was nameless when Oinomaos ruled,
And drenched with many a snowstorm.
In this first birthday-rite
The Fates stood near at hand,
And he who alone proves the very truth,

Time. In his forward march
He has revealed all clearly:
How Herakles portioned the booty, war's gift,
Made sacrifice and founded
The fourth year's feast
With the first Olympiad
And the winning of victories.

The evening was lit
By the lovely light of the fair-faced moon.

All the holy place was loud with song
In the glad feasting like the music of banquets.

(LINES 43–58 and LINES 74–77)

VIEW OF ATHENS WITH LYCABETTUS AND HYMETTUS IN THE BACKGROUND
by Henry Cook. c. 1850. Oil on canvas.
Vouros-Eutaxias Museum of the City of Athens

MOUNT HYMETTUS (FROM ART OF LOVE, BOOK III)
Ovid (43 B.C.–A.D. 17)

TRANSLATED BY WILLIAM CONGREVE

Near, where his purple head Hymettus shows
And flow'ring hills, a sacred fountain flows,
With soft and verdant turf the soil is spread,
And sweetly-smelling shrubs the ground o'ershade.
There rosemary and bays their odours join,
And with the fragrant myrtle's scent combine.
There tamarisks with thick-leav'd box are found,
And cytisus and garden-pines abound.
While through the boughs, soft winds of Zephyr pass,
Tremble the leaves and tender tops of grass.
Hither would Cephalus retreat to rest,
When tir'd with hunting, or with heat opprest;
And, thus, to Air, the panting youth would pray:
'Come, gentle Aura, come, this heat allay'.

(LINES 686–699)

OLIVE TREE
Lorenzo Mavilis (1860–1912)
TRANSLATED BY RAE DALVEN

In your hollow, hoary olive tree,
nests a bee-hive, bending with a fillet
of green still wound about you
as if to adorn you like a corpse.

And each little bird chirping
in love's giddiness starts
an amorous chase on your bough
on your boughs that will never bud again.

Oh now the beauties of lively youth
will sweeten you in death
with the magic sounds they make,

multiplying in you like memories;
ah, if other souls could die like this,
sisters of your soul.

Olive Tree.
1950s.
Benaki Museum, Athens. Photographic Archive
Photograph: Voula Papaioannou

Labyrinth on a coin from Knossos.
c. 350–280 B.C.
Silver stater.
Numismatic Museum, Athens.
Photograph: TAP Service, Athens

THE LABYRINTH (FROM ATLAS)

Jorge Luis Borges (1899–1986)

TRANSLATED BY ANTHONY KERRIGAN

This is the labyrinth of Crete. This is the labyrinth of Crete whose center was the Minotaur. This is the labyrinth of Crete whose center was the Minotaur that Dante imagined as a bull with a man's head in whose stone net so many generations were as lost as Maria Kodama and I were lost. This is the labyrinth of Crete whose center was the Minotaur that Dante imagined as a bull with a man's head in whose stone net so many generations were as lost as Maria Kodama and I were lost that morning, and remain lost in time, that other labyrinth.

Representation of Rhodes on a silver tetradrachm.
Mid-4th century B.C.
Numismatic Museum, Athens.
Photograph: TAP Service, Athens

RHODES (from OLYMPIAN, 7)
Pindar (c. 438 B.C.)

TRANSLATED BY FRANK J. NISETICH

Ancient stories tell us
that when Zeus and the gods
were allotting the world,
Rhodes was not yet visible on the ocean surface—
it lay hidden,
an island in the briny depths.

And Helios was absent—no one assigned him a portion,
  he was left without a place,
    even he, the sacred god.
      Then at his complaint
        Zeus would have cast the lots
                  a second time,
      but Helios forbade it,
     saying he had seen
    within the gray depths, growing
  from the sea's floor, an island
that would be
           rich in nurture for men and kindly to their flocks.

He told Lachesis, garlanded in gold, to raise her hands
  and swear never to break
    the gods' great oath,
      but nod assent with Zeus
        that once Rhodes
              had broken through
     to bright air,
    it would be his prize.
   He spoke, and what he said
  came, in truth,
to fulfillment:
        the sea's glittering furrows put forth
the island,
       and now the father, source of piercing light
and master of fire-breathing horses
has her for his own.

(LINES 54–73)

TRIPLETS FOR BEAUTIFUL MISTRA

Nikos Karouzos (1926–1990)

TRANSLATED BY PHILIP SHERRARD

On the clay of the Greeks lowly gleaming
Mistra like an innocent passion
reposes its dead in the sun.

Pantánassa, the evening light
pours through your coloured windows
the scent of stars.

How joy moistens the early leaves
and dew glints on a stone ascent—
the eagle of glory alone on the floor of Byzantine beauty.

There I recall John's city
and weightless pavements blue
in the reflection of the Attic twilight.

Bitter road leading to what is past,
flowering apple-trees moving up to God,
susurrating poplars, the sky's pyx.

And in outdoor forgetfulness, O humble mud-brick cottage,
the skull of a bus
in the wall's shadow.

Caught are we all in the sky's trap—
the numberless apple-trees, phial-like churches, the spring
as a woman's womb outside in the fatherland.

I inhale the smoke of burning laurel:
aloft in the inhabited sky alone
knowing the divine joy of the elements.

I appease the wind with laments
as the vetch stirs desolate
and pinks wound with the scent of festivals.

I left my love in her body, I became a journey.
Gazing deeply into her hair beyond time
I do not exist, stabs upon her hair.

Ruined palaces like women unknown and blind:
vanity
gains the terror of beauty.

Take the oil-lamp, you who will guide our thirst—
the hour is as a funeral pyre—
in the night of Mistra drink with us of this hyacinth.

Behold Taygetus at night over the kastro
while the sky proclaims the sea's blueness
and cries are heard from invisible dogs.

What do you wait for, Greek, facing the stars?
Pain was made for you and beauty
was given you like water great and endless.

TO ZANTE
Ugo Foscolo (1778–1827)

TRANSLATED BY EDGAR ALLAN POE

Fair isle, that from the fairest of all flowers,
Thy gentlest of all gentle names dost take!
How many memories of what radiant hours
At sight of thee and thine at once awake!
How many scenes of what departed bliss!
How many thoughts of what entombed hopes!
How many visions of a maiden that is
No more,—no more upon thy verdant slopes!
No more! alas, that magical, sad sound
Transforming all! Thy charms shall please no more
Thy memory no more! Accursed ground
Henceforth I hold thy flower-enamelled shore,
O hyacinthine isle! O purple Zante!
'Isola d'oro! Fior di Levante!'

SOUVENIR DE ZANTE by Künzli frères, Zürich.
Early 20th century. Postcard.
Courtesy Greek Literary and Historical Archives Society (ELIA), Athens

HYMN ON THE MORNING OF CHRIST'S NATIVITY
John Milton (1608–1674)

The Oracles are dumm,
No voice or hideous humm
   Runs through the arched roof in words deceiving.
Apollo from his shrine
Can no more divine,
   With hollow shriek the steep of Delphos leaving.
No nightly trance, or breathed spell,
Inspire's the pale-ey'd priest from the prophetic cell.

The lonely mountains o'er,
And the resounding shore,
   A voice of weeping heard, and loud lament;
From haunted spring, and dale
Edg'd with poplar pale,
   The parting Genius is with sighing sent,
With flowre-inwov'n tresses torn
The Nimphs in twilight shade of tangled thickets mourn.

The Temple of Apollo, Delphi.
1950s.
Benaki Museum, Athens. Photographic Archive
Photograph: Voula Papaioannou

Mountains and Sea.
Photograph: Courtesy Greek National Tourist Organization, Athens

FROM MYTHISTOREMA [MYTHICAL STORY]
George Seferis (1900–1971)
TRANSLATED BY EDMUND KEELEY AND PHILIP SHERRARD

10

Our country is enclosed, all mountains
which have the low sky for a roof day and night.
We have no rivers, we have no wells, we have no springs,
only a few cisterns—and these empty—which echo and which we
　　worship.
A sound stagnant, hollow, the same as our loneliness
the same as our love, the same as our bodies.
We find it strange that once we were able to build
our houses, huts, and sheepfolds.
And our marriages, the cool coronals and the fingers
become enigmas inexplicable to our soul.
How were our children born, how did they grow?

Our country is enclosed. The two black
Symplegades enclose it. When we go down
to the harbours on Sunday to breathe
we see, alight in the sunset,
the broken timbers of voyages unfinished
bodies that no longer know how to love.

THE SEA

ULYSSES IN THE SEA (FROM THE ODYSSEY, BOOK V)
Homer (? 9th century B.C.)

TRANSLATED BY ROBERT FITZGERALD

A great wave drove at him with toppling crest
spinning him round, in one tremendous blow,
and he went plunging overboard, the oar-haft
wrenched from his grip. A gust that came on howling
at the same instant broke his mast in two,
hurling his yard and sail far out to leeward.
Now the big wave a long time kept him under,
helpless to surface, held by tons of water,
tangled, too, by the seacloak of Kalypso.
Long, long, until he came up spouting brine,
with streamlets gushing from his head and beard;
but still bethought him, half-drowned as he was,
to flounder for the boat and get a handhold
into the bilge—to crouch there, foiling death.
Across the foaming water, to and fro,
the boat careered like a ball of tumbleweed
blown on the autumn plains, but intact still.
So the winds drove this wreck over the deep,
East Wind and North Wind, then South Wind and West,
coursing each in turn to the brutal harry.

(LINES 330–350)

THE WRECK OF ODYSSEUS'S SHIP (detail),
by Hagesandros, Polydoros, and Athenodoros, from Grotto at Sperlonga.
2nd century B.C.–1st century A.D.
Marble.
Museo Archeologico Nazionale, Sperlonga.
Photograph: Deutsches Archaologisches Institut, Rome

Detail of a mermaid holding a ship and a fish. Courtyard of J. Yoyce, Spetsae Island. Mid-19th century. Pebble mosaic.
Photograph: Courtesy National Bank of Greece

OF THE AEGEAN (FROM ORIENTATIONS)
Odysseus Elytis (Born 1911)
TRANSLATED BY KIMON FRIAR

Love	Love	Love
The archipelago	Its song	Its ship
And the prow of its foam	And the horizons of its voyage	And the freedom from care of its etesian winds
And the seagull of its dream	And the echo of its nostalgia	And the jib of its hope
On its highest mast the sailor waves	On love's wettest rock the betrothed awaits	On its highest undulation an island rocks
A song	A ship	The homecoming

BOAT by Costas Tsoclis.
1982.
Boat, wood, paint.
Pinacotheki Dimitri Pieridis, Athens

FROM AGAMEMNON (IN THE ORESTEIA)
Aeschylus (525–456 B.C.)

TRANSLATED BY ROBERT FAGLES

The Island of Santorini.
1950s.
Benaki Museum, Athens. Photographic Archive
Photograph: Voula Papaioannou

IMPRESSION DU VOYAGE
Oscar Wilde (1856–1900)

The sea was sapphire coloured, and the sky
    Burned like a heated opal through the air,
    We hoisted sail; the wind was blowing fair
For the blue lands that to the eastward lie.
From the steep prow I marked with quickening eye
    Zakynthos, every olive grove and creek,
    Ithaca's cliff, Lycaon's snowy peak,
And all the flower-strewn hills of Arcady.
The flapping of the sail against the mast,
    The ripple of the water on the side,
    The ripple of girls' laughter at the stern,
The only sounds:—when 'gan the West to burn,
    And a red sun upon the seas to ride,
    I stood upon the soil of Greece at last!

Detail from a votive clay tablet with a scene of a warship.
From the sanctuary of Athena at Sounion.
Early 7th century B.C.
National Archaeological Museum, Athens.
Photograph: TAP Service, Athens

THE ARGONAUTS
D. H. Lawrence (1885–1930)

They are not dead, they are not dead!
Now that the sun, like a lion, licks his paws
and goes slowly down the hill:
now that the moon, who remembers, and only cares
that we should be lovely in the flesh, with bright, crescent feet,
pauses near the crest of the hill, climbing slowly, like a queen
looking down on the lion as he retreats—

Now the sea is the Argonauts' sea, and in the dawn
Odysseus calls the commands, as he steers past those foamy islands;
wait, wait, don't bring the coffee yet, nor the *pain grillé.*
The dawn is not off the sea, and Odysseus' ships
have not yet passed the islands, I must watch them still.

SANTORINI by Constantinos Maleas.
Early 20th century.
Oil on canvas.
National Gallery, Alexandros Soutzos Museum, Athens

ODE TO SANTORINI

Odysseus Elytis (Born 1911)

TRANSLATED BY EDMUND KEELEY AND PHILIP SHERRARD

You came out of the thunder's belly
Shuddering in the penitential clouds
Bitter stone, tested, defiant
You summoned the sun to be your first witness
To confront with you the impetuous radiance
To open out with a crusading echo in the sea

Sea-woken, defiant,
You thrust up a breast of rock
Scored with the south wind's inspiration
For pain to engrave its guts there
For hope to engrave its guts there
With fire, lava, smoke
With words that concert the infinite
You gave birth to the voice of day
You raised,
To the green and rose porticos of vision,

The bells struck by the exalted intellect
Praising the birds in the mid-August light.

Close to the wave's thud, to the foam's lament,
Among the eucharists of sleep
When night wandered through the wilderness of stars
Searching for the testimony of dawn
You experienced the joy of birth.

You were the first to leap forth into the world,
Porphyrogenite, sea-begotten,
You sent to the far horizons
Blessings nurtured in the sea's vigils
To caress the hair of daylight's waking hour.

Queen of the heartbeats, and wings of the Aegean,
With words that convert the infinite
With fire, lava, smoke,
You discovered the great lines of your destiny.

Now justice stands revealed before you
Black mountains sail in the brightness
Longings dig their craters
In the heart's tormented land
And from hope's struggle a new earth is made ready
So that on a morning full of iridescence
The race that vivifies dreams
The race that sings in the sun's embrace
May stride forth with eagles and banners.

O daughter of the highest wrath
Sea-begotten, naked,
Open the glorious gates of man
So that health may sweeten the land
The senses may flower in a thousand colours
Their wings spread wide
So that freedom may blow from all directions.

In the wind's proclamation flash out
The new, the eternal beauty
When the three-hour-old sun rises up
Entirely blue to play the harmonium of creation.

CHIOS
Ioanna Tsatsos (Born 1919)
TRANSLATED BY JEAN DEMOS

On rocky Chios . . . (Homeric Hymn to Apollo)

Let me whisper into a shell of your sea
A verse in your praise island of Faith
Your waves carry Niobe's sigh
From the opposite shore
Their salt made bitter by her tears

Let me sing you a verse island of Homer
How I saw your pomegranate trees rising up
At midday
Each Byzantine dome a pomegranate
Embroidered in tile
Countless embellished domes
Nostalgic memories of the exiled emperor
Who rode up your slopes
Climbed your peaks
Marking the cliffs with his vow.

Now we pilgrims to Byzantium
Follow his tracks
Marveling in the woods at the little fires
That illumine the ikon of Our Lady
As it answers the grief of Niobe.

The Village of Anavoti on the Island of Chios.
Photograph: Courtesy Greek National Tourist Organization, Athens

Terrace of the Lions, Delos.
7th century B.C.
Naxian marble.
Photograph: Courtesy Greek National Tourist Organization, Athens

DELOS (FROM THE AEGEAN AND THE ISLANDS)
Lawrence Durrell (1912–1990)

On charts they fall like lace,
Islands consuming in a sea
Born dense with its own blue:
And like repairing mirrors holding up
Small towns and trees and rivers
To the still air, the lovely air:
From the clear side of springing Time,
In clement places where the windmills ride,
Turning over grey springs in Mykonos,
In shadows with a gesture of content.

The statues of the dead here
Embark on sunlight, sealed
Each in her model with the sightless eyes:
The modest stones of Greece,
Who gravely interrupted death by pleasure.

And in harbours softly fallen
The liver-coloured sails—
Sharp-featured brigantines with eyes—
Ride in reception so like women:
The pathetic faculty of girls
To register and utter a desire
In the arms of men upon the new-mown waters,
Follow the wind, with their long shining keels
Aimed across Delos at a star.

FROM MYTHISTOREMA [MYTHICAL STORY]
George Seferis (1900–1971)
TRANSLATED BY EDMUND KEELEY AND PHILIP SHERRARD

Argonauts

And if the soul
is to know itself
it must look
into a soul:
the stranger and enemy, we've seen him in the mirror.

The companions were good men, they never complained
about the work or the thirst or the frost,
they had the bearing of trees and waves
that accept the wind and the rain
accept the night and the sun
without changing in the midst of change.
They were good men, whole days
they sweated at the oars with lowered eyes
breathing in rhythm
and their blood reddened a submissive skin.
Sometimes they sang, with lowered eyes
as we were passing the dry island with the Barbary figs
to the west, beyond the cape
of the barking dogs.
If it is to know itself, they said
it must look into a soul, they said
and the oars struck the sea's gold
in the sunset.
We passed many capes many islands the sea
leading to another sea, gulls and seals.
Sometimes unfortunate women wept
lamenting their lost children
and others raging sought Alexander the Great
and glories buried in the depths of Asia.
We moored on shores full of night-scents
with the singing of birds, waters that left on the hands
the memory of great happiness.
But the voyages did not end.
Their souls became one with the oars and the oarlocks
with the solemn face of the prow
with the rudder's wake
with the water that shattered their image.
The companions died in turn,
with lowered eyes. Their oars
mark the place where they sleep on the shore.

No one remembers them.   Justice.

The Island of Mykonos.
1940s.
Benaki Museum, Athens. Photographic Archive
Photograph: Voula Papaioannou

The Island of Mykonos.
1980.
Photograph: Tony Stone Worldwide

FROM DON JUAN (CANTO III, LXXXVI, I)
Lord Byron (1788–1824)

The isles of Greece, the isles of Greece!
    Where burning Sappho loved and sung,
Where grew the arts of war and peace,—
    Where Delos rose, and Phoebus sprung!
Eternal summer gilds them yet,
But all, except their sun, is set.

THE HERITAGE

THE DEATH OF DIGENIS

Anonymous Folk Song
(18th century version of Byzantine period original)
TRANSLATED BY RICHARD STONEMAN

Digenis is wrestling for his soul, earth trembles at his struggle.
The heaven thunders, lightnings flash, the upper world is shaking,
The world below has opened up, it cracks to its foundations,
The paving stones are shuddering: how shall they cover him?
How shall they cover the hero up, the eagle of the earth?
His house could not contain him, even the caves were found too small,
He stepped over the mountain slopes, he jumped across their peaks,
He played bowls with the mountain crags, he crushed the foothills flat,
He seized the young birds in their nests, the adults on the wing,
The deer and the wild mountain goats he captured on the run.
Charos is envious of the man, he watches from afar:
He has taken hold of Digenis' heart, he has entrapped his soul.

DIGENIS by Spiros Vassiliou.
1943.
Woodcut.
Collection the artist

ΔΙΓΕΝΗΣ

Stage set by Yannis Pappas for the performance of Aeschylus's "The Suppliant Women"
in the ancient theater of Epidaurus. Produced by the National Theater of Greece.
1964.
Photograph: Collection the artist

THE SUPPLIANT WOMEN
Euripides (c. 480–406 B.C.)
TRANSLATED BY FRANK JONES

                                    Nothing
Is worse for a city than an absolute ruler.
In earliest days, before the laws are common,
One man has power and makes the law his own:
Equality is not yet. With written laws,
People of small resources and the rich
Both have the same recourse to justice. Now
A man of means, if badly spoken of,
Will have no better standing than the weak;
And if the little man is right, he wins
Against the great. This is the call of freedom:
"What man has good advice to give the city,
And wishes to make it known?" He who responds
Gains glory; the reluctant hold their peace.
For the city, what can be more fair than that?

                                    (LINES 428–442)

WAR HYMN
Rhigas Pheraios (1759–1798)
TRANSLATED BY RAE DALVEN

How long, my heroes, shall we live in bondage,
alone like lions on ridges, on peaks?
Living in caves, seeing our children
turned from the world to bitter enslavement?
Losing our land, brothers, and parents,
our friends, our children and all our relations?
Better an hour of life that is free
than forty years in slavery!

In the east, west, south and north,
let all have one heart for one land.
Let each worship God in the fashion he pleases,
let us hasten together to the glory of war,
let each whom tyranny has exiled
now return to his own.
Bulgarians, Albanians, Armenians, Greeks,
black and white, let us belt the sword
all together in a surge for freedom,
so the world will know that we are the brave!
How did our forefathers surge like lions,
leaping for liberty into the fire?
So we, brothers too, must seize our arms
and cast off at once this bitter slavery,
to slay the wolves who impose the yoke,
and cruelly torture Christian and Turk.
Let the Cross shine on land and sea,
let justice make the enemy kneel,
let the world be healed of this grievous wound,
and let us live on earth as brothers—free.

MAP OF GREECE by Rhigas Velestinlis (Pheraios).
1797.
Engraving.
Gennadius Library, Athens

THE RIGHTEOUS DECISION OF GOD FOR THE LIBERATION OF GREECE by Panagiotis Zographos. From the portfolio, WAR OF INDEPENDENCE IN PICTURES, commissioned by General Makriyannis. 1836–39. Watercolor on board. *Gennadius Library, Athens*

ODE TO LIBERTY
Dionysios Solomos (1798–1857)

TRANSLATED BY RUDYARD KIPLING

We knew thee of old,
O divinely restored,
By the light of thine eyes
And the light of thy Sword.

From the graves of our slain
Shall thy valour prevail
As we greet thee again—
Hail, Liberty! Hail!

Long time didst thou dwell
Mid the peoples that mourn,
Awaiting some voice
That should bid thee return.

Ah, slow broke that day
And no man dared call,
For the shadow of tyranny
Lay over all:

From the graves of our slain
Shall thy valour prevail
As we greet thee again—
Hail, Liberty! Hail!

Study for MASSACRE AT CHIOS
(LES MASSACRES DE SCIO)
by Eugène Delacroix.
1824. Watercolor.
Musée du Louvre, Paris.
Photograph: © Photo RMN

HELENA
Alfred de Vigny (1797–1863)
TRANSLATED BY RICHARD STONEMAN

Hear, hear that solitary bell
Ringing from the peak of desolate Scio.
Its clangour, full of sombre ecstasy,
Brings armed men from the mountains to the port:
The winds have risen now for vengeance,
And the night is excited with their knowledge.
Greek scarlet covers their brows
Like the innocent purple which adorns
The heads of choirboys
When mass is said at our altars.
This sign is fixed to the warriors' foreheads.
Who will dare to flee or stay in hiding?
Lighted tapers gleam and smoke in their hands;
The air is aflame as from a distant fire:
The sable of the sea shows its gilded flanks,
And high on the mountains the cedars flash.
The crowds are on the shore, their eager hope
Casts glances on the tumbling waves in vain,
When, with a friendly whistle from the dark,
A rebel ship emerges from the shadows.
A bloody standard slaps around its pole.
An astonishing number of armed warriors
Pours on to its three gangways: the cannon
Which flashes from its porthole repeats its thunder.
Cries greet it, cries are returned:
The hymn of slaughtered Rigas echoes round:
The impatient tocsin's rebellious note
Sounds liberty from the roof of the chapel.
Assembling, excitement, arming and being armed;
At the sound the eagle leaves its rock in terror.

BYRON (dressed in Greek costume).
Artist unknown. c. 1850.
Oil on canvas.
Benaki Museum, Athens

FROM CHILDE HAROLD'S PILGRIMAGE (CANTO II, LXXXVIII)
Lord Byron (1788–1824)

Where'er we tread 'tis haunted, holy ground;
No earth of thine is lost in vulgar mould
But one vast plain of wonder spreads around,
And all the Muse's tales seem truly told,
Till the sense aches with gazing to behold
The scenes our earliest dreams have dwelt upon. . . .

HEAD by Yannis Ritsos.
c. 1967–73.
Drawing on stone.
Collection the artist.
Photograph: Platonas Maximos

FROM ROMIOSINI
Yannis Ritsos (1909–1991)
TRANSLATED BY PHILIP PASTRAS AND GEORGE PILITSIS

I

Those trees are not made for a lesser sky,
those rocks are not made for the heels of strangers,
those faces are made only for the sun,
those hearts are made only for justice.

This place is as harsh as silence,
clasps its fiery stones to its breast,
clasps in light its orphaned olive trees and vineyards,
clenches the teeth. There is no water—only light.
The road is lost in light and the shadow of the wall is iron.
Trees, rivers and voices have turned to marble in the whitewash
    of the sun.

The root stumbles on the marble. The dusty lentisks.
The mule and the rock. They gasp. No water.
All are thirsty. For years now. All chew a mouthful of sky to
    choke down their bitterness.
Their eyes are red from the vigil
a deep line wedged between their eyebrows
like a cypress between two mountains at sunset.

Their hand is glued to the gun
the gun is an extension of their arm
their arm is an extension of their soul—
they have wrath upon their lips
and grief, deep deep within their eyes,
like a star in a salt pit.

When they tighten their grip, the sun is certain for the world
when they smile, a small swallow flees from within their fiery
    beards
when they sleep, twelve stars fall from their empty pockets
when they are killed, life marches up high with banners and with
    drums.

For so many years all are hungry, all are thirsty, all are killed
besieged by land and sea,
scorching heat devoured their fields and the brine drenched their
    houses
the wind knocked down their doors and the few lilac trees in the
    square
death comes and goes through the holes in their overcoats
their tongues are as acrid as cypress cones
their dogs died wrapped in their shadows
the rain beats down on their bones.

Stone-still in their lookouts, they smoke cow dung and the night
and keep watch over the frenzied sea where
the broken mast of the moon has sunk.

The bread gone, the bullets gone
now they load their cannons only with their hearts.

So many years besieged by land and sea
all are starved, all are killed, and no one has died—
in their lookouts their eyes glow
an enormous banner, an enormous fire flame-red
and at every dawn thousands of doves soar out of their hands
toward the four gates of the horizon. . . .

60

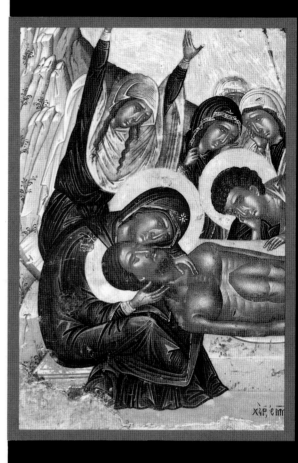

FROM EPITAPHIOS
Yannis Ritsos (1909–1991)
TRANSLATED BY KIMON FRIAR

. . . .
A day in May you left me, a day in May I lose you,
springtime, son, when you loved to go up

To the terrace and look out, and with your eyes
you'd milk the light of the universe without ever getting your fill,

And with your pointed finger you'd show me one by one
all that was sweet, all that was good and pale and rosy,

And you'd show me the sea gleaming in the distance like oil,
and the trees and mountains in the azure veil,

And the poor small things—birds, ants, shrubs,
and these diamond stones which the water jug nearby would sweat.

And yet, my son, although you'd show me the stars and the vastness,
I'd see them more clearly in your sea-blue eyes.

And with a voice that was sweet and warm and manly
you'd tell me of more things than the grains of sand on the shore,

And you'd tell me, my son, that all this beauty would be ours,
and now you are dead, and dead are our glow and our flame. . . .

LAMENT by Emmanuel Lombardos.
First half of the 17th century (Cretan school).
Tempera on wood panel.
Byzantine Museum, Athens

61

THE ALTAR OF THE FATHERLAND
Andreas Kalvos (1792–1869)

TRANSLATED BY PHILIP SHERRARD

Hurry, brothers, hurry,
eager, courageous souls;
around the fatherland's
altar shining
hurry always.

Let disunity cease,
disunity which throws the nations,
blindly, beneath the harshest
claws of sleepless
treacherous tyrants.

Hurry here; in concord
let us weave the dance,
each one offering
splendid precious sacrifice
to the fatherland.

Here let us readily
purify our passions;
let us seize arms
only to wound
the Mussulman's breast.

Let us pour here
all our wealth; while
we hold the naked sword,
laurel's honoured leaves
suffice us.

And then, when we have shattered
the most hated yoke,
freedom again will give us
other rewards, not
uncertain riches.

Here, friends, let us forsake
pleasure and rest;
a hard stone is the mattress
and poison the bread
of slavery.

Here, as votive offerings,
close beside the altar,
brethren, our children,
loved ones and the elders
now let us leave.

Whatever our heart
most precious holds, it is not fit
for men who cower
before the senseless
barbarian sceptre.

Nor is life fit.
Hurry, brothers, hurry.
In measure let us dance,
in measure let us die
for the fatherland.

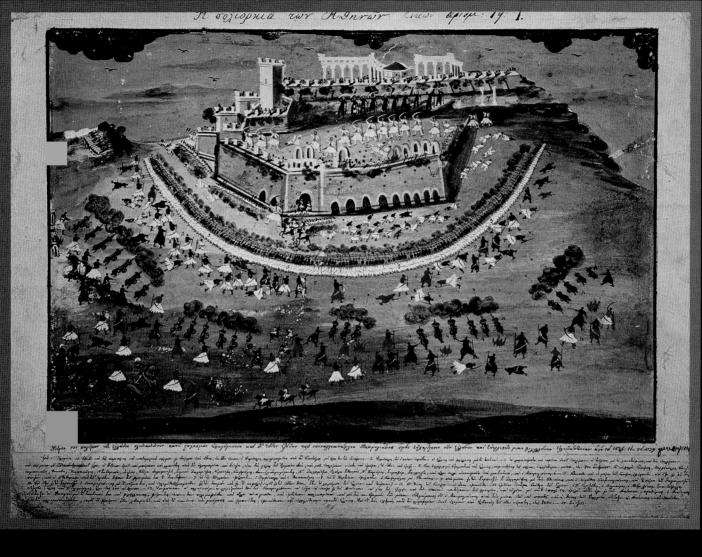

THE SIEGE OF ATHENS by Panagiotis Zographos. From the portfolio,
THE WAR OF INDEPENDENCE IN PICTURES, commissioned by General Makriyannis.
1836–39. Watercolor on board.
Gennadius Library, Athens

Tank invading Polytechnical School, Athens.
November 17, 1973.
Photograph: Alecos Voutsaras

PROTEST

THE POLYTECHNIC. NOVEMBER 1973.

Ioanna Tsatsos (Born 1919)

TRANSLATED BY JEAN DEMOS

I have no way to fight the tanks
Perhaps on some just day
All that remains will be the flute.

Lightning stretched in the darkness
The young left their books left love
And they pushed forward
In their big eyes
Truth
Death

Terror was choking the air

From the bare walls
The shades of the dead gave orders.
I wanted to cry out:
'But I am alive
The blood from my wound is warm.'
The red horse galloped ahead

"And to that one was given a sword."

At the peak of the night under its lights
Man facing his God
Man facing his own kind his hangman.

The groans in that cell a nightmare.

I put my ear to the ground
I listened to the thud of horses
Galloping to forestall
The depth of this moment.
I sense it the horrible happening
Which silence conceals.
Sin punishes the earth
It furrows the mountains
It opens up caves
Dust upon dust the dead on their horses.

In the eyes of the young duty and death.

In other times we admired courage
When they fought and died man to man
The land now is haunted
With iron machines.

Now I know
I shall not see the world again as before
The good time has set
The spotless foam of the waves is stained
The pebbles on the beach are dull
The warmth of the sun a vain thing.

And this spring this strange paper spring
How can I embrace it?
It is not mine
Its radiance is all on the surface
The lilies the crocuses colorless spindly
Wither with the young who have left us
They do not respond to the light.

I hate the virtue of husbandry
Glory is nothing to me
What I keep is the cyclamen.
The moist fragrance of autumn
You are all that remains you call me
To touch the tune that fashioned the Lekythos.

Waves of the ocean
Gales of the earth
All are moving against me
And with them my soul.

I am tired of the murmur of seeking water
I am tired of the protest of sufferers
Just let me sleep on the white stone.

AKATHISTOS HYMN
Anonymous (5th century)
TRANSLATED BY CONSTANTINE A. TRYPANIS

To you, Mother of God, champion and leader, I, your city [Constantinople],
delivered from sufferings, ascribe the prize of victory and my thanks. And may
you, in your invincible power, free me from all kinds of dangers, that I may cry
to you: "Hail, wedded maiden and virgin."

"Hail to you through whom joy will shine out;
hail to you through whom the curse shall pass away;
hail, redemption of fallen Adam;
hail, deliverance of the tears of Eve;
hail, height unattainable by human thought;
hail, depth invisible even to the eyes of angels;
hail to you, the throne of the king;
hail to you who bear him, the bearer of all;
hail, start that heralds the sun;
hail, womb of divine incarnation;
hail to you through whom creation is reborn;
hail to you through whom the Creator becomes a child;
hail, wedded maiden and virgin."

FROM AXION ESTI
Odysseus Elytis (Born 1911)
TRANSLATED BY EDMUND KEELEY AND GEORGE SAVIDIS

HAIL Girl Burning and hail Girl Verdant
Hail Girl Unrepenting, with the prow's sword

Hail you who walk and the footprints vanish
Hail you who wake and the miracles are born

Hail O Wild One of the depths' paradise
Hail O Holy One of the islands' wilderness

Hail Mother of Dreams, Girl of the Open Seas
Hail O Anchor-bearer, Girl of the Five Stars

Hail you of the flowing hair, gilding the wind
Hail you of the lovely voice, tamer of demons

Hail you who ordain the Monthly Ritual of the Gardens
Hail you who fasten the Serpent's belt of stars.

Hail O Girl of the just and modest sword
Hail O Girl prophetic and daedalic

Hagia Sophia, Constantinople, by Anthemius of Tralles and Isidorus of Miletus.
A.D. 532–37.
Photograph: G. E. Kidder Smith, New York

DESCRIPTION OF HAGIA SOPHIA

Paul the Silentiary (c. A.D. 563)

TRANSLATED BY RICHARD STONEMAN

The roof is made of golden-plated tiles
From which a sparkling blaze of gold sends beams
No more supportable to human eyes
Than Phaethon at his noon-day halt in spring,
When every crag is bleached gold. Yes, my king,
When he had brought the whole world to agree,
And gathered wealth from Rome, and native wealth,
Thought no stone honour worthy of the temple
Of great, immortal God, in whom proud Rome
Had placed her hopes entirely. Silver too
He did not stint to pour forth. Sunium's crag
And Mount Pangaeum bled their silver veins
And treasured heaps of mighty kings were broached.
Where, in the east, the great perimeter
Enclosed the shrine of bloodless sacrifice,
No ivory, no bronze or carved stone stood,
But all the aisle was lined with brightest silver.
Not only on the sanctuary walls,
Where the initiate is enthroned, but even
The columns were entirely cased in silver,
Shining with leaping light, a dozen strong.

THE LAST MASS IN HAGIA SOPHIA

Anonymous Song of Lamentation
for the Fall of Constantinople in 1453

TRANSLATED BY RICHARD STONEMAN

God rings the bells, earth rings the bells, the sky itself is ringing,
The Holy Wisdom, the great church, is ringing out the message,
Four hundred sounding boards sound out, and two and sixty bells,
For every bell there is a priest, for every priest a deacon.
To the left the emperor is singing, to the right the patriarch,
And all the columns tremble with the thunder of the chant.
And as the emperor began the hymn to the Cherubim,
A voice came down to them from the sky, from the archangel's mouth:

Cease the Cherubic hymn, and let the sacred objects bow;
Priests, take the holy things away, extinguish all the candles:
God's Will has made our city now into a Turkish city.
But send a message to the West, and let them send three ships:
The first to take the cross, the second to remove the Gospel,
The third, the finest shall rescue for us our holy altar,
Lest it fall to those dogs, and they defile it and dishonour it.
The Holy Virgin was distressed, the very icons wept.
Be calm, beloved Lady, be calm and do not weep for them:
Though years, though centuries shall pass, they shall be yours again.

THE FALL OF CONSTANTINOPLE by Panagiotis Zographos. From the portfolio, THE WAR OF INDEPENDENCE IN PICTURES, commissioned by General Makriyannis. 1836–39. Watercolor on board.
Gennadius Library, Athens

PATMOS
Friedrich Hölderlin (1770–1843)

TRANSLATED BY DAVID GASCOYNE

The God is near, and
                       difficult to grasp.
But danger fortifies the rescuing power.
In sombre places dwell the eagles; the Alps' sons
Go fearless forth upon the roads of the abyss
Across lightly constructed bridges. And since all round there press
The peaks of time, and those so close
In love, are worn out on the separate heights,
Then give us the innocent waters,
O give us wings, that with the truest thought
We may fly yonder and return to this same place.

I spoke thus. And then rose
A guardian spirit, carried me away
More swiftly and still further than I dreamed,
Far from my house and home.
And as I passed, the light of dawn
Glowed on the shady woods and longed-for streams
Of my own land. I knew the earth no more.
And soon, with mysterious freshness shining
And rapidly growing beneath the footsteps of the sun,
In golden haze there blossomed forth
In a thousand peaks, a thousand glittering spires,

Asia, before my eyes. I blindly sought
For some familiar image,
A stranger to those wide streets where there descends
From Tmolus to the sea the Pactolus adorned with gold
And the Taurus rises with the Messogis,
And the flowering garden like a peaceful fire,
But in the light on high, the silver snow
And sign of immortal life, on the unscaled wall
The age-old ivy grows, and on living pillars
Of cedar and of laurel
Stand the solemn palaces the Gods have built.

And all around the Asiatic gates,
Calling out here and there from the sea's uncertain plain,
There murmur the unshadowed roads.
But the pilot knows the islands.
When I hear
That Patmos was among the nearest isles,
I longed to disembark
And to approach its gloomy caves.

Bell Towers of the Monastery of St. John the Theologian, Patmos.
1986.
Photograph: © David Beatty

For it is not like Cyprus rich with springs
Or any of the other islands, it is not
In proud display that Patmos stands
But like a poor house full of hospitality,
And when from a wrecked ship, or weeping
For his lost land or for an absent friend
A stranger comes, she listens with good will;
And all her children, and the voices of the hot groves,
And the place where the sand falls, and where the fields are cracked,
And all the sounds
Hear him, and all resounds again
With love for the man's plaint.
Thus it was one day that she took in care
The belov'd of God, the seer
Who in his happy youth had gone
With the All-Highest's Son, inseparable from Him.

THE PEOPLE

THERE IS NO JOY WITHOUT APHRODITE
Mimnermus (630 B.C.)

TRANSLATED BY RICHMOND LATTIMORE

What, then, is life if love the golden is gone? What is pleasure?
  Better to die when the thought of these is lost from my heart:
the flattery of surrender, the secret embrace in the darkness.
  These alone are such charming flowers of youth as befall
women and men. But once old age with its sorrows advances
  upon us, it makes a man feeble and ugly alike,
heart worn thin with the hovering expectation of evil,
  lost all joy that comes out of the sight of the sun.
Hateful to boys a man goes then, unfavored of women.
  Such is the thing of sorrow God has made of old age.

45/100   Ghika

FROM ANNIVERSARY
Odysseus Elytis (Born 1911)
TRANSLATED BY EDMUND KEELEY AND PHILIP SHERRARD

> *. . . even the weariest river*
> *winds somewhere safe to sea.*

I brought my life this far
To this spot that struggles
Always near the sea
Youth on rocks, breast
To breast against the wind
Where a man may go
Who is nothing else but a man
Summing up his green moments
With coolness, the visions of his hearing
With waters, his remorses with wings
Ah, Life
Of a child who becomes a man
Always near the sea when the sun
Teaches him to breathe toward that place where
The shadow of a seagull vanishes.

I brought my life this far
White summation, black total
A few trees and a few
Wet pebbles
Light fingers to caress a forehead
What forehead
Anticipations wept all night and are no more
There is no one
That a free footstep might be heard
That a voice may dawn refreshed
That sterns may splash by quays, inscribing
A name of deeper azure on their horizon
A few years, a few waves
Sensitive rowing
In the bays surrounding love.

KOUROS by Odysseus Elytis
1978.
Collage.
Collection the artist

FROM PROMETHEUS
Aeschylus (525–456 B.C.)
TRANSLATED BY DAVID GRENE

Bright light, swift-winged winds, springs of the rivers, numberless
laughter of the sea's waves, earth, mother of all, and the all-seeing
circle of the sun: I call upon you to see what I, a God, suffer
at the hands of Gods—
see with what kind of torture
worn down I shall wrestle ten thousand
years of time—
such is the despiteful bond that the Prince
has devised against me, the new Prince
of the Blessed Ones. Oh woe is me!
I groan for the present sorrow,
I groan for the sorrow to come, I groan
questioning when there shall come a time
when He shall ordain a limit to my sufferings.
What am I saying? I have known all before,
all that shall be, and clearly known; to me,
nothing that hurts shall come with a new face.
So must I bear, as lightly as I can,
the destiny that fate has given me;
for I know well against necessity,
against its strength, no one can fight and win.

I cannot speak about my fortune, cannot
hold my tongue either. It was mortal man
to whom I gave great privileges and
for that was yoked in this unyielding harness.
I hunted out the secret spring of fire,
that filled the narthex stem, which when revealed
became the teacher of each craft to men,
a great resource. This is the sin committed
for which I stand accountant, and I pay
nailed in my chains under the open sky.

Ah! Ah!
What sound, what sightless smell approaches me,
God sent, or mortal, or mingled?
Has it come to earth's end
to look on my sufferings,
or what does it wish?
You see me a wretched God in chains,
the enemy of Zeus, hated of all
the Gods that enter Zeus's palace hall,
because of my excessive love for Man.

(LINES 88–123)

Scene from the production of "Prometheus Bound" by Aeschylus, in the ancient theater of Delphi. Produced by Angelos Sikelianos. Costumes by Eva Palmer Sikelianos. 1929. *Benaki Museum, Athens. Photographic Archive. Photograph: Nelly's*

FROM ANTIGONE
Sophocles (490–406 B.C.)
TRANSLATED BY ROBERT FAGLES

CHORUS:

                                    Numberless wonders
terrible wonders walk the world but none the match for man—
that great wonder crossing the heaving gray sea,
                    driven on by the blasts of winter
on through breakers crashing left and right,
    holds his steady course
and the oldest of the gods he wears away—
the Earth, the immortal, the inexhaustible—
as his plows go back and forth, year in, year out
    with the breed of stallions turning up the furrows.

And the blithe, lightheaded race of birds he snares,
the tribes of savage beasts, the life that swarms the depths—
                    with one fling of his nets
woven and coiled tight, he takes them all,
    man the skilled, the brilliant!
He conquers all, taming with his techniques
the prey that roams the cliffs and wild lairs,
training the stallion, clamping the yoke across
    his shaggy neck, and the tireless mountain bull.

And speech and thought, quick as the wind
and the mood and mind for law that rules the city—
    all these he has taught himself
and shelter from the arrows of the frost
when there's rough lodging under the cold clear sky
and the shafts of lashing rain—
            ready, resourceful man!
                    Never without resources
never an impasse as he marches on the future—
only Death, from Death alone he will find no rescue
but from desperate plagues he has plotted his escapes.

Man the master, ingenious past all measure
past all dreams, the skills within his grasp—
    he forges on, now to destruction
now again to greatness. When he weaves in
the laws of the land, and the justice of the gods
that binds his oaths together
            he and his city rise high—
                    but the city casts out
that man who weds himself to inhumanity
thanks to reckless daring. Never share my hearth
never think my thoughts, whoever does such things.

                                    (LINES 376–416)

Man.
1930s.
Benaki Museum, Athens. Photographic Archive
Photograph: Nelly's

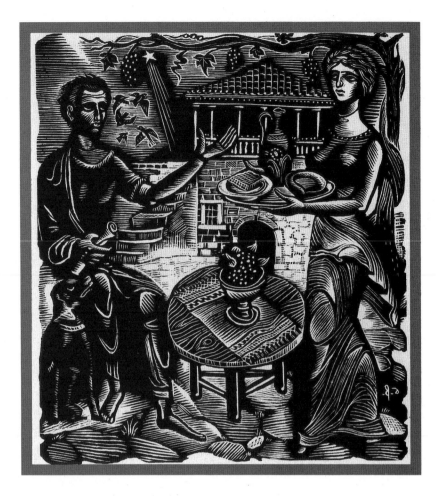

Illustration by Spiros Vassiliou for the poem, "Thalero."
1940s. Woodcut. *Estate of the artist*

THALERO
Angelos Sikelianos (1884–1951)

TRANSLATED BY EDMUND KEELEY AND PHILIP SHERRARD

Glowing, festive, warm, the moon looked down
    over the vineyards
while the sun still scorched the bushes, setting
    in total stillness.

The heavy grass up on the windless height sweated
    its pungent sap
and from the new-leaved vines that climbed
    the terraced slope

the vine-keepers whistled and waved, the robins
    hovered nearby
and the heat spread a fine filmy veil across
    the moon's face.

On the path between the wheat fields three oxen,
    one behind the other,
ascended the mountain slope, their pendant
    dewlaps swaying.

The slender hound, his muzzle to the earth
    in the quiet evening,
leapt from rock to rock, searching
    for my tracks.

And at the house ahead, beneath the unripe vine,
    a ready table
waited for me, a lamp hung out in front of it—
    the evening star.

There the master's daughter brought me honeycomb, cold water,
            country bread;
her strength had engraved around her rock-like throat a circle
            like a dove's ring;

and her look, like the evening light, disclosed virginity's
            lucid flame,
and through the tight dress that covered her firm breasts the nipple
            stood out boldly.

Her hair was plaited in two braids
            above her forehead—
braids like the cables of a ship, too thick
            for my hand's grip.

The dog, exhausted now from the steep footpaths,
            stood there panting,
and, motionless, stared into my eyes,
            waiting for a crust.

There, as I heard the nightingale and ate fruit from the dish
            in front of me,
I had the taste of wheat, of song and honey
            deep on the palate.

As in a glass hive my soul moved inside me,
            a joyful bee-swarm
that, secretly increasing, seeks to release into the trees
            its grape-like cluster.

And I felt the earth as crystal beneath my feet,
            the soil transparent,
for the strong and peaceful bodies of young plane-trees
            rose up around me.

There the old wine was opened for me, smelling rich
            in the porous jar,
as mountain scents when the cool night dew
            falls on the bushes.

Glowing, festive, warm, there my heart consented
            to repose for a while
in sheets made fragrant by herbs, azure
            by washing blue.

FROM THE BACCHAE
Euripides (c. 480–406 B.C.)
TRANSLATED BY WILLIAM ARROWSMITH

—What is wisdom: What gift of the gods
   is held in honor like this:
   to hold your hand victorious
   over the heads of those you hate?
   Honor is precious forever.

—Blessèd is he who escapes a storm at sea,
     who comes home to his harbor.
—Blessèd is he who emerges from under affliction.
—In various ways one man outraces another in the
     race for wealth and power.
—Ten thousand men possess ten thousand hopes.
—A few bear fruit in happiness; the others go awry.
—But he who garners day by day the good of life,
     he is happiest. Blessèd is he.

(LINES 897–910)

THE MIRACULOUS FINDING OF THE SERVANT
by Emanuel Lombardos. A story from the Synaxary of St. Minas.
Miniature from the border of an icon of St. Minas.
First half of the 17th century, Venice.
Hellenic Institute of Byzantine and Post-Byzantine Studies of Venice.
Photograph: Courtesy National Bank of Greece, Athens

LOVE

ANTIGONE by Nikos Hatzikyriakos-Ghikas.
1955.
Aquatint.
Collection the artist

FROM ANTIGONE
Sophocles (496–406 B.C.)
TRANSLATED BY ROBERT FAGLES

CHORUS:

Love, never conquered in battle
Love the plunderer laying waste the rich!
Love standing the night-watch
              guarding a girl's soft cheek,
you range the seas, the shepherds' steadings off in the wilds—
not even the deathless gods can flee your onset,
nothing human born for a day—
whoever feels your grip is driven mad.

(LINES 879–886)

"TO AN ARMY WIFE, IN SARDIS . . ."

Sappho (c. 600 B.C.)

TRANSLATED BY MARY BARNARD

To an army wife, in Sardis:

Some say a cavalry corps,
some infantry, some, again,
will maintain that the swift oars

of our fleet are the finest
sight on dark earth; but I say
that whatever one loves, is.

This is easily proved: did
not Helen—she who had scanned
the flower of the world's manhood—

choose as first among men one
who laid Troy's honor in ruin?
warped to his will, forgetting

love due her own blood, her own
child, she wandered far with him.
So Anactoria, although you

being far away forget us,
the dear sound of your footstep
and light glancing in your eyes

would move me more than glitter
of Lydian horse or armored
tread of mainland infantry.

ARCHAIC HEAD IV by Roy Lichtenstein.
1988. Patinated Bronze.
© Roy Lichtenstein.
Courtesy Castelli Gallery.
Photograph: © Dorothy Zeidman 1989

88

from MEDEA
Euripides (480–406 B.C.)
TRANSLATED BY REX WARNER

Of all things which are living and can form a judgment
We women are the most unfortunate creatures.
Firstly, with an excess of wealth it is required
For us to buy a husband and take for our bodies
A master; for not to take one is even worse.
And now the question is serious whether we take
A good or bad one; for there is no easy escape
For a woman, nor can she say no to her marriage.
She arrives among new modes of behavior and manners,
And needs prophetic power, unless she has learned at home,
How best to manage him who shares the bed with her.
And if we work out all this well and carefully,
And the husband lives with us and lightly bears his yoke,
Then life is enviable. If not, I'd rather die.
A man, when he's tired of the company in his home,
Goes out of the house and puts an end to his boredom
And turns to a friend or companion of his own age.
But we are forced to keep our eyes on one alone.
What they say of us is that we have a peaceful time
Living at home, while they do the fighting in war.
How wrong they are! I would very much rather stand
Three times in the front of battle than bear one child.

(LINES 230–251)

Melina Mercouri in the play "Medea," by Euripides. Produced by the State Theater of Northern Greece. 1976.
Photograph: Courtesy Melina Mercouri

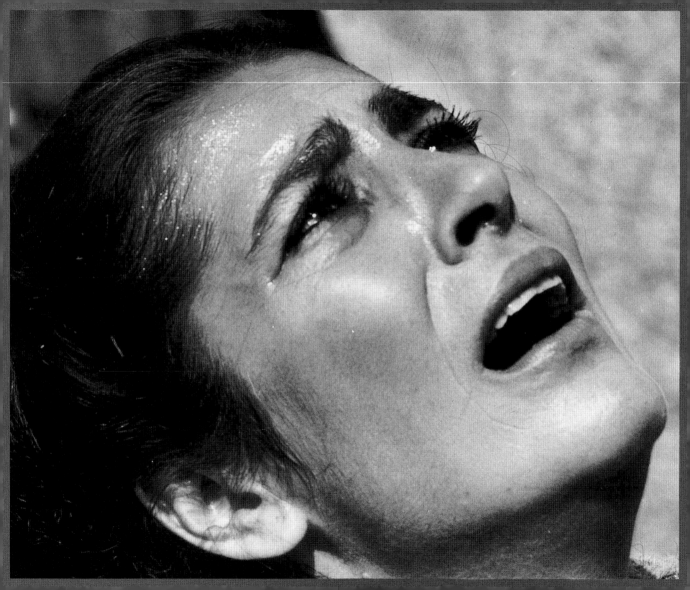

FROM AGAMEMNON (IN THE ORESTEIA)
Aeschylus (525–456 B.C.)
TRANSLATED BY ROBERT FAGLES

CLYTEMNESTRA

         For me, the tears that welled
like springs are dry. I have no tears to spare.
I'd watch till late at night, my eyes still burn,
I sobbed by the torch I lit for you alone.

I never let it die . . . but in my dreams
the high thin wail of a gnat would rouse me,
piercing like a trumpet—I could see you
suffer more than all
the hours that slept with me could ever bear.

I endured it all. And now, free of grief,
I would salute that man the watchdog of the fold,
the mainroyal, saving stay of the vessel,
rooted oak that thrusts the roof sky-high,
the father's one true heir.
Land at dawn to the shipwrecked past all hope,
light of the morning burning off the night of storm,
the cold clear spring to the parched horseman—
O the ecstasy, to flee the yoke of Fate!

It is right to use the titles he deserves.
Let envy keep her distance. We have suffered
long enough.

              (LINES 877–897)

BRIDAL SONGS
Sappho (c. 600 B.C.)
TRANSLATED BY SUZY Q. GRODEN

Happy bridegroom!
Now your wedding has come true,
as you have prayed, and you have
the girl for whom you prayed.
You are a joy to look at,
with your gentle eyes,

and love showers down about
your handsome face . . .
Aphrodite has honored you
above all others . . .

a bride: Childhood, my childhood, where
are you going when you leave me?

childhood: I'll never come to you again,
never, never.

HYMEN by Georges Braque. Named after Hymenaeus, a deity of marriage.
1939, cast executed later. Bronze.
Courtesy the Patsy R. and Raymond D. Nasher Collection, Dallas, Texas

FROM EROTOCRITOS
Vizentzos Cornaros (16TH–17TH CENTURY)
TRANSLATED BY THEODORE P. STEPHANIDES

Observe how Eros works his magic spells,
And how all love-sick mortals he compels.
He quickens their desire and gives it might,
And teaches them to wrestle in the night.
He cheapens gold, to blemish he gives charm.
And to the weakling lends a warrior's arm;
He makes the coward dare, the sluggard race,
The awkward he endows with every grace.
Love made Rotocritos to hold his ground
And to defy the ten who gathered round.

(LINES 543–552)

Ρωμέο και
Ιουλία

PENELOPE'S DESPAIR
Yannis Ritsos (1909–1991)

TRANSLATED BY EDMUND KEELEY

It wasn't that she didn't recognize him in the light from the
    hearth; it wasn't
the beggar's rags, the disguise—no. The signs were clear:
the scar on his knee, the pluck, the cunning in his eye. Frightened,
her back against the wall, she searched for an excuse,
a little time, so she wouldn't have to answer,
give herself away. Was it for him, then, that she'd used up
    twenty years,
twenty years of waiting and dreaming, for this miserable
blood-soaked, white-bearded man? She collapsed voiceless into a
    chair,
studied the slaughtered suitors on the floor as though seeing
her own desires dead there. And she said "Welcome" to him,
hearing her voice sound foreign, distant. In the corner, her loom
covered the ceiling with a trellis of shadows; and all the birds she'd
    woven
with bright red thread in green foliage, now,
this night of the return, suddenly turned ashen and black,
flying low on the level sky of her final enduring.

RETURN OF ULYSSES by Nikos Engonopoulos.
1947.
Oil on canvas.
Collection Lena Engonopoulos, Athens

BLIND EROS BETWEEN TWO SIRENS by Defterevontos Sifnou.
1825. Oil on wood.
Byzantine Museum, Athens

THE ALPHABET OF LOVE
Anonymous Folk Song (EARLY 19TH CENTURY)
TRANSLATED BY THEODORE STEPHANIDES

A

At your sweet smile the heavens gleam and hills and valleys bloom;
Sunbeams are woven from your hair as on a golden loom.

B

Before your door a blade of grass grew in the morning light,
But you did crush it, cruel maid, beneath your foot so white.

C

Could you but look into my heart, O maiden sweet and fair,
As in a mirror you would see your face reflected there.

D

Do you remember how one night we watched the full moon rise,
And, lip to lip, we never knew when dawn had kissed the skies!

E

Endure, my heart, the cruel words of her whom you have lost,
Endure them as the hills endure the chill winds and the frost.

F

For five long years I courted you, yet you have spurned my suit;
I wooed, alas! a lemon tree—and plucked its bitter fruit.

G

Gone is the time, O heartless one, when you my love could spurn;
Aye, for another now I sigh—sigh you for me in turn!

H

How can I face the mocking world that points at me with scorn?
For I am wounded once again—and by the selfsame thorn!

I

I haunt the spot when last we kissed beside the fountain clear,
A lingering echo of that kiss I hope that I may hear.

J

Jerusalem or Mecca lure the pilgrim from afar,
But I am lured by your bright eyes as by a holy star.

K

King, golden-crowned, the rising sun has put the shades to flight;
The east drips with the crimson blood of Love's accomplice, Night.

L

Life is a golden apple tree and Love its blossoms gay,
And Death a robber of the night who steals the fruit away.

M

My love is like the frozen drift that on Olympus glows:
Before the summer sun can thaw, another winter snows.

N

No more shall sing Love's nightingale from Life's sweet myrtle bough;
For on the cruel ground it lies, slain by a broken vow.

O

O stab me with a dagger sharp, but spare my heart alone—
For you are shrined within that heart and you may wound your own.

P

Proud maid, the rose tree by your gate with cruel spell you blast;
A rosebud dies of jealousy each day as you go past.

Q

Queen are you of all my heart; why do you refrain
From turning Love's enchanted key to enter your domain!

R

Red roses still retain their scent though sere they be and dry;
And likewise shall my love endure when cold in death I lie.

S

Sweet maiden, you have every gift of beauty and of grace.
And I thank Him Who gave me eyes by which to see your face.

T

The youth who meets you passing by and feels no passion grow,
May lightning smite him! For naught else can set his blood aglow.

U

Ungainly pitcher by the well, would I could take your place;
You know her lips against your lip, you feel her arms' embrace!

V

Vile is the tongue that rails at Love, and viler still the heart
That, fearful of so sweet a wound, would flinch from Love's keen dart.

W

Why does your mother light a lamp when daylight fades and dies,
Since, brighter than the moon and stars, she has your shining eyes!

X

Xeromero and Agrapha, the mountains and the sea,
Stand witness to my steadfast love and intercede for me.

Y

You pass me by indifferently, proud maid, each time we meet;
But *other* trees bear oranges that beckon just as sweet.

Z

Zoë, the springtime of my eyes, my heart's midsummer goal,
The autumn of my withered hopes, the winter of my soul!

THE THREE GODDESSES (HESTIA, DIONE, AND APHRODITE), East pediment, Parthenon. c. 438–432 B.C. Marble.
British Museum, London. Photograph: Hirmer Verlag, Munich

"WITH HIS VENOM . . ."
Sappho (c. 600 B.C.)
TRANSLATED BY MARY BARNARD

With his venom

Irresistible
and bittersweet

that loosener
of limbs, Love

reptile-like
strikes me down

"THANK YOU, MY DEAR . . ."
Sappho (c. 600 B.C.)
TRANSLATED BY MARY BARNARD

Thank you, my dear

You came, and you did
well to come: I needed
you. You have made

love blaze up in
my breast—bless you!
Bless you as often

as the hours have
been endless to me
while you were gone

IN SPRING
Ibykos (c. 560 B.C.)

TRANSLATED BY DIANE J. RAYOR

In Spring, quince trees
irrigated with streams
from rivers, in the Virgins'
inviolate garden, and vinebuds
growing beneath shady shoots
of vinetwigs bloom. But for me
Love rests for no season:
blazing with lightning
Thracian Boreas,
darting from Kypris, dark
with parching madness, shameless,
violently shakes
my senses from the depth.

DAPHNIS AND CHLOE by Marc Chagall. 1957–58.
Original color lithograph for the book *Daphnis and Chloe*
Museum Theophilos, Collection Tériade, Varia, Mytilini (Lesbos)

DESPINA by Yannis Tsarouhis.
1968.
Oil on canvas.
Yannis Tsarouhis Foundation, Athens

AMORGOS
Nicos Gatsos (1911–1992)

TRANSLATED BY EDMUND KEELEY AND PHILIP SHERRARD

VI

How very much I loved you only I know
I who once touched you with the eyes of the Pleiades,
Embraced you with the moon's mane, and we danced on the
    meadows of summer
On the harvest's stubble, and together ate cut clover,
Great dark sea with so many pebbles round your neck, so
    many colored jewels in your hair. . . .

For years and years, O my tormented heart, have I struggled
    with ink and hammer,
With gold and fire, to fashion an embroidery for you,
The hyacinth of an orange tree,
A flowering quince tree to comfort you—
I who once touched you with the eyes of the Pleiades,
Embraced you with the moon's mane, and we danced on the
    meadows of summer
On the harvest's stubble, and together ate cut clover.
Great dark loneliness with so many pebbles round your neck,
    so many colored jewels in your hair.

BETRAYAL
Anonymous Folk Song (EARLY 19TH CENTURY)
TRANSLATED BY PHILIP SHERRARD

Night it was, dear, when we kissed:
Who could have seen us?
It was the night and dawn that saw,
It was the moon and stars.
A star leant down and told the sea,
The sea, it told the oar,
The oar spoke to the sailor, and
The sailor went and sang it
At the window of his love.

THE KISS by Nikiphoros Lytras.
1875.
Oil on canvas.
National Gallery, Alexandros Soutzos Museum, Athens.
Collection Euripides Koutlidis

A GREEK WEDDING by Louis Dupré.
1821.
Lithograph.
Benaki Museum, Athens

THE VILLAGE WEDDING

Angelos Sikelianos (1884–1951)

TRANSLATED BY EDMUND KEELEY AND PHILIP SHERRARD

The bride sits
on a low polished stool,

she looks neither right nor left
as the bridesmaids,
standing behind her back,
part her hair in the middle
along the crown of her head,
and when they have combed it through,
shaken it out into the air,
powerfully,
with three fingers separating
the soft treasure,

their quiet hands begin
to braid the plaits
like slings
one on top of the other.
(Let the breeze from the door
bathe the basil-leaved herb
that grows in the mountain air
as it hangs in the blue shade
from the great beam of the house,

or the dry flying-fish,
its wings outspread,
balanced high
in this sailor's home,
exposed to every wind that blows,
like the caique
of the bride's seafaring father
to the breath of God.

Nailed to the white walls
let the interwoven wheatears gleam,

and from the one window to the other
let the swallow fly
quick as lightning.

But around the bride, motionless,
covered now with the delicate headdress,
let the crystal silence pour,

and let her virginal thought flow
as on grassy slopes,
in the windless sun,
the wild pear tree unfolds its flowers.)

Do you listen within your veil,
silent, God-quickened heart?

There it is, the first tread of the mules
scattering the stones as they come.

But riding a stallion, leading the way, the bridegroom
greets all creation as his dowry.

ANDROMACHE AND HECTOR by Giorgio de Chirico.
1986, after original of 1940.
Bronze.

ACHILLES AND PRIAM (FROM THE ILIAD, BOOK XXIV)
Homer (? 9th century B.C.)

TRANSLATED BY ROBERT FAGLES

ANDROMACHE AND HECTOR

                "O my husband . . .
cut off from life so young! You leave me a widow,
lost in the royal halls—and the boy only a baby,
the son we bore together, you and I so doomed.
I cannot think he will ever come to manhood.
Long before *that* the city will be sacked,
plundered top to bottom! Because you are dead,
her great guardian, you who always defended Troy,
who kept her loyal wives and helpless children safe,
all who will soon be carried off in the hollow ships
and I with them—
                And you, my child, will follow me
to labor, somewhere, at harsh, degrading work,
slaving under some heartless master's eye—that,
or some Achaean marauder will seize you by the arm
and hurl you headlong down from the ramparts—horrible death—
enraged at you because Hector once cut down his brother,
his father or his son, yes, hundreds of armed Achaeans
gnawed the dust of the world, crushed by Hector's hands!
Your father, remember, was no man of mercy . . .
not in the horror of battle, and that is why
the whole city of Troy mourns you now, my Hector—
you've brought your parents accursed tears and grief
but to me most of all you've left the horror, the heartbreak!
For you never died in bed and stretched your arms to me
or sent some last word from the heart I can remember
always weeping for you through all my nights and days."

                  (LINES 850–878)

LULLABY
Anonymous Folk Song (EARLY 19TH CENTURY)
TRANSLATED BY PHILIP P. ARGENTI AND H. N. ROSE

My little baby sleeps, the little birds sleep,
The tame ones, the wild ones and the little swallows.

Sleep, lucky one, sleep, well-omened one,
Whom your mother has brought up on caresses.

Sleep, for I have ordered your dowry from Constantinople,
Your clothes and your diamonds from Venice.

My only child, my only little offspring is sleeping,
The one leaf of my heart and the one apple of my eye.

THE LAMENT
Anonymous Folk Song (EARLY 19TH CENTURY)
TRANSLATED BY MARGARET ALEXIOU

What shall I send you, my dear one, there in the Underworld?
If I send an apple, it will rot, if a quince, it will shrivel;
if I send grapes, they will fall away, if a rose, it will droop.
So let me send my tears, bound in my handkerchief.

Lamenting Women, Island of Karpathos.
1960s.
Photograph: Constantine Manos / Magnum

THE CUP

Anacreon (563–478 B.C.)

TRANSLATED BY THOMAS STANLEY

Vulcan come, thy hammer take,
And of burnish'd silver make
(Not a glittering armour, for
What have we to do with war?)
But a large deep bowl, and on it
I would have thee carve (no planet:
Pleiads, Wains, or Waggoners,
What have we to do with stars?)
But to life exactly shape
Clusters of the juicy grape;
Whilst brisk Love their bleeding heads
Hand in hand with Bacchus treads.

AN EVENING SONG
Alcaeus (c. 600 B.C.)

TRANSLATED BY JAMES S. EASBY-SMITH

Let us drink, and pledge the night!
Wherefore wait the torches' light?
  Twilight's hour is brief.
Pass the ample goblet 'round,
Gold-enwrought, whereon is wound
  Many a jewelled leaf.
Sprung from Semele and Zeus
Dionysus gave to us
  Care-dispelling wine.
Pouring out the liquid treasure
With one part of water measure
  Two parts from the vine.
Mix it well, and let it flow,
Cup on cup shall headlong go,
  While we drink and laugh,
  While we sing and quaff.

Silver oenochoe (wine jar) with the head of Silenus,
from the Tomb of Philip, Vergina, Macedonia.
350–325 B.C.
Archaeological Museum, Thessaloniki.
Photograph: TAP Service, Athens

Detail of a KYLIX showing a symposium scene by the "Antiphon Painter."
490–480 B.C.
Nicholas P. Goulandris Foundation-Museum of Cycladic Art, Athens

FROM DON JUAN (CANTO III, LXXXVI, 15 AND 16)
Lord Byron (1788–1824)

Fill high the bowl with Samian wine!
    Our virgins dance beneath the shade—
I see their glorious black eyes shine;
    But gazing on each glowing maid,
My own the burning tear-drop laves,
To think such breasts must suckle slaves.

Place me on Sunium's marbled steep—
    Where nothing, save the waves and I,
May hear our mutual murmurs sweep;
    There, swan-like, let me sing and die:
A land of slaves shall ne'er be mine—
Dash down yon cup of Samian wine!

OUZO UNCLOUDED
Robert Graves (1895–1986)

Here is ouzo (she said) to try you:
Better not drowned in water,
Better not chilled with ice,
Not sipped at thoughtfully,
Nor toped in secret.
Drink it down (she said) unclouded
At a blow, this tall glass full,
But keep your eyes on mine
Like a true Arcadian acorn-eater.

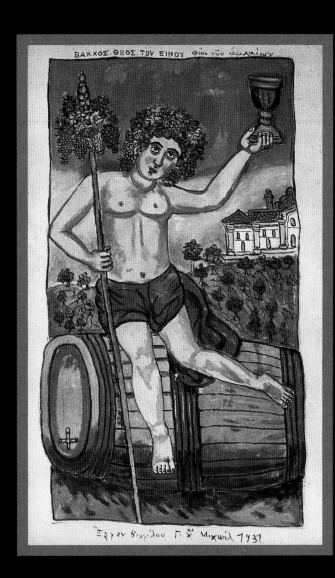

BACCHUS, THE GOD OF WINE by Theophilos.
c. 1939.
Watercolor.
Theophilos Museum, Collection Tériade, Varia, Mytilini (Lesbos).
Photograph: Courtesy Greek National Tourist Organization, Athens

SUMMER (FROM WORKS AND DAYS)
Hesiod (c. 800 B.C.)

TRANSLATED BY RICHMOND LATTIMORE

Keep away from sitting in the shade or lying in bed
    till the sun's up
in the time of the harvest, when the sunshine
    scorches your skin dry.
This is the season to push your work and bring home
    your harvest;
get up with the first light so you'll have enough
    to live on.
Dawn takes away from work a third part
    of the work's measure.
Dawn sets a man well along on his journey,
    in his work also,
dawn, who when she shows, has numerous people going
    their ways; dawn who puts the yoke upon many oxen.
But when the artichoke is in flower,
    and the clamorous cricket
sitting in his tree lets go his vociferous singing,
    that issues
from the beating of his wings, in the exhausting
    season of summer;
then is when goats are at their fattest,
    when the wine tastes best,
women are most lascivious, but the men's strength
    fails them
most, for the star Seirios shrivels them, knees
    and heads alike,
and the skin is all dried out in the heat; then,
    at that season,
one might have the shadow under the rock,
    and the wine of Biblis,
a curd cake, and all the milk that the goats
    can give you,
the meat of a heifer, bred in the woods,
    who has never borne a calf,
and of baby kids also. Then, too, one can sit
    in the shadow
and drink the bright shining wine, his heart
    satiated with eating
and face turned in the direction where Zephyros
    blows briskly,
make three libations of water from a spring
    that keeps running forever
and has no mud in it; and pour wine
    for the fourth libation.

(LINES 573–593)

Harvest in Summer. 1930s. *Benaki Museum, Athens. Photographic Archive. Photograph: Nelly's*

FAREWELL FOLK SONG

Anonymous (EARLY 19TH CENTURY)

TRANSLATED BY LORING N. DANFORTH

"My little bird, far away in a foreign land, sad and with a heavy heart,
that foreign land rejoices in your presence, and I drink poison.
What should I send you Eleni? What should I order for you?
If I send an apple, it will rot. If I send a quince, it will shrivel up.
If I send basil, without water it will wither.
I will send you a tear in a linen handkerchief."
But my tear was burning hot, and it dyed the handkerchief black.
I washed it in nine rivers, but I could not restore its color.
Then I washed it in a shallow stream, and I did restore its color.
But a partridge flew down to drink from the stream, and its wings
    were dyed black.

ΕΘΝΙΚΗ ΑΤΜΟΠΛΟΪΑ ΤΗΣ ΕΛΛΑΔΟΣ

NATIONAL STEAM NAVIGATION Cᴼ Lᴛᴅ. OF GREECE

Η ΤΑΧΥΤΕΡΑ ΕΞ ΕΛΛΑΔΟΣ ΚΑΤ᾽ ΕΥΘΕΙΑΝ ΔΙ᾽ ΑΜΕΡΙΚΗΝ ΓΡΑΜΜΗ

PATRIS (HOMELAND), the transatlantic oceanliner
that transported Greek immigrants to the United States.
Early 20th century.
Lithograph.
Courtesy Greek Literary and Historical Archives Society (ELIA), Athens

WARRIOR WITH SHIELD.
Reproduced from Guy Davenport.
ARCHILOCHUS, SAPPHO, ALKMAN: Davenport.
Copyright © 1980
The Regents of the University of California

THE SHIELD

Archilochus (c. 750–650 B.C.)

TRANSLATED BY H.D.F. KITTO

Some lucky Thracian has my noble shield:
I had to run; I dropped it in a wood.
But I got clear away, thank God! So hang
The shield! I'll get another, just as good.

Photograph of the performance, "Peace" by Aristophanes,
at the Greek Art Theater, Athens. Directed by Karolos Koun.
Set and costumes by Dionissis Fotopoulos. 1977.
Photograph: Courtesy Greek Art Theater

ABOUT "PEACE" (FROM PAEAN)
Bacchylides (505–450 B.C.)

TRANSLATED BY ROBERT FAGLES

Not only that,
But Peace regenerates man
As her wealth refines,
And her blooms of song unfurl;
Fires fed by thighs of bulls
And the woolly sheep
Flicker on crafted shrines
And leap to Olympus;
Young ones tumble to games
And the rounds of reeds and rites.

Through shield-grips cased in iron
The glistening spiders lash their warps;
Barbed spears, double-edge swords—
Sacked by the bite of rust; . . .
No horns blast their brass bells,
No eyes are looted of genial sleep
That warms hearts ripe
An hour before the sun streams high—
But roads reel with our revels of love
And exuberant ballads of boys flare up.

INTERLUDE OF JOY

George Seferis (1900–1971)

TRANSLATED BY EDMUND KEELEY AND PHILIP SHERRARD

That whole morning we were full of joy,
my God, how full of joy.
First, stones leaves and flowers shone
then the sun
a huge sun all thorns and so high in the sky.
A nymph collected our cares and hung them on the trees
a forest of Judas trees.
Young Loves and satyrs played there and sang
and you could see pink limbs among the black laurels
bodies of little children.
The whole morning long we were full of joy;
the abyss a closed well
tapped by the tender hoof of a young faun.
Do you remember its laugh—how full of joy!
Then clouds rain and the wet earth.
You stopped laughing when you lay down in the hut
and opened your large eyes as you watched
the archangel practicing with a fiery sword—
"Inexplicable," you said, "inexplicable.
I don't understand people:
no matter how much they play with colors
they are all black."

FESTIVITY ON THE SEASHORE II by Nikos Hatzikyriakos-Ghikas.
1931.
Oil on canvas.
National Gallery and Alexandros Soutzos Museum, Athens

Photograph of Yannis Papaioannou, second from left in foreground,
playing a bouzouki at a taverna in Tzitzifies (Athens).
1952.

NIGHTS I STAY AWAKE WITHOUT HOPE [Rebetiko]

By Yannis Papaionnou (1913–1972)

TRANSLATED BY GAIL HOLST

Nights I stay awake without hope.
Lonely, I walk the streets.
In front of the bars of your window
I spend my sad hours.

How I long to meet you again,
To find our old joy once more,
To give you my kisses again
So my black sadness will leave me.

But there where you are in a strange place,
Who knows where you wander now?
I wonder if you still think of me
Or suffer for someone else.

THE PICTURE
Anacreon (563–478 B.C.)

TRANSLATED BY THOMAS STANLEY

Painter, by unmatch'd desert
Master of the Rhodian art,
Come, my absent mistress take,
As I shall describe her: make
First her hair, as black as bright,
And if colours so much right
Can but do her, let it too
Smell of aromatic dew;
Underneath this shade, must thou
Draw her alabaster brow;
Her dark eye-brows so dispose
That they neither part nor close
But by a divorce so slight
Be disjoin'd, may cheat the sight:
From her kindly killing eye
Make a flash of lightning fly,
Sparkling like Minerva's, yet
Roses in milk swimming seek
For the pattern of her cheek:
In her lip such moving blisses,
As from all may challenge kisses;
Round about her neck (outvying
Parian stone) the Graces flying;
And o'er all her limbs at last
A loose purple mantle cast;
But so ordered that the eye
Some part naked may descry,
An essay by which the rest
That lies hidden may be guess'd.
    So, to life th' hast come so near,
    All of her, but voice, is here.

GIRL PAINTING by Yannis Moralis.
1971.
Diptych. Acrylic on canvas.
Private collection.
Photograph: Courtesy the artist

THE SPIRIT

FROM HELLAS, A LYRIC DRAMA
Percy Bysshe Shelley (1792–1822)

. . . . But Greece and her foundations are
Built below the tide of war
Based on the crystalline sea
Of thought and its eternity.
Her citizens, imperial spirits,
Rule the present from the past. . . .

The world's great age begins anew,
The golden years return,
The earth doth like a snake renew
Her winter weeds outworn. . . .

A brighter Hellas rears its mountains
From waves serener far;
A new Peneus rolls his fountains
Against the morning-star. . . .

Another Athens shall arise . . .

Detail of the Bosphorus Sea and Constantinople,
Schwartz Mansion, Ambelakia. 1798. Fresco.
Photograph: Courtesy National Bank of Greece

SAILING TO BYZANTIUM

WILLIAM BUTLER YEATS (1865–1939)

I

That is no country for old men. The young
In one another's arms, birds in the trees
—Those dying generations—at their song,
The salmon-falls, the mackerel-crowded seas,
Fish, flesh, or fowl, commend all summer long
Whatever is begotten, born, and dies.
Caught in that sensual music all neglect
Monuments of unageing intellect.

II

An aged man is but a paltry thing,
A tattered coat upon a stick, unless
Soul clap its hands and sing, and louder sing
For every tatter in its mortal dress,
Nor is there singing school but studying
Monuments of its own magnificence;
And therefore I have sailed the seas and come
To the holy city of Byzantium.

III

O sages standing in God's holy fire
As in the gold mosaic of a wall,
Come from the holy fire, perne in a gyre,
And be the singing-masters of my soul.
Consume my heart away; sick with desire
And fastened to a dying animal
It knows not what it is; and gather me
Into the artifice of eternity.

IV

Once out of nature I shall never take
My bodily form from any natural thing,
But such a form as Grecian goldsmiths make
Of hammered gold and gold enamelling
To keep a drowsy Emperor awake;
Or set upon a golden bough to sing
To lords and ladies of Byzantium
Of what is past, or passing, or to come.

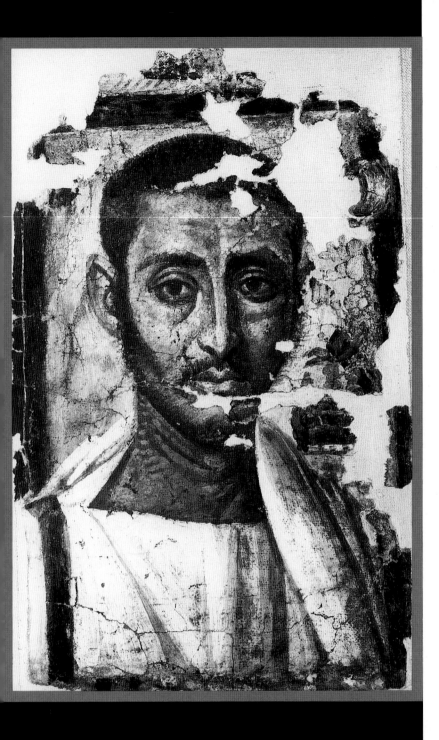

PORTRAIT OF A YOUNG MAN.
Mid-3rd century A.D.
Fayyum, encaustic on linen.
Benaki Museum, Athens

AS MUCH AS YOU CAN
Constantine Cavafy (1863–1933)
TRANSLATED BY EDMUND KEELEY
AND PHILIP SHERRARD

Even if you can't shape your life
    the way you want,
at least try as much as you can
not to degrade it
by too much contact with the world,
by too much activity and talk.

Do not degrade it by dragging it along,
taking it around and exposing it so often
to the daily silliness
of social relations and parties,
until it comes to seem a boring hanger-on.

ITHAKA
Constantine Cavafy (1863–1933)
TRANSLATED BY EDMUND KEELEY AND PHILIP SHERRARD

As you set out for Ithaka
hope your road is a long one,
full of adventure, full of discovery.
Laistrygonians, Cyclops,
angry Poseidon—don't be afraid of them:
you'll never find things like that on your way
as long as you keep your thoughts raised high,
as long as a rare excitement
stirs your spirit and your body.
Laistrygonians, Cyclops,
wild Poseidon—you won't encounter them
unless you bring them along inside your soul,
unless your soul sets them up in front of you.

Hope your road is a long one.
May there be many summer mornings when,
with what pleasure, what joy,
you enter harbors you're seeing for the first time;
may you stop at Phoenician trading stations
to buy fine things,
mother of pearl and coral, amber and ebony,
sensual perfume of every kind—
as many sensual perfumes as you can;
and may you visit many Egyptian cities
to learn and go on learning from their scholars.

Keep Ithaka always in your mind.
Arriving there is what you're destined for.
But don't hurry the journey at all.
Better if it lasts for years,
so you're old by the time you reach the island,
wealthy with all you've gained on the way,
not expecting Ithaka to make you rich.

Ithaka gave you the marvellous journey.
Without her you wouldn't have set out.
She has nothing left to give you now.

And if you find her poor, Ithaka won't have fooled you.
Wise as you will have become, so full of experience,
you'll have understood by then what these Ithakas mean.

PAINTED COMMENTS by Yannis Moralis. Illustrations for *The Poems of George Seferis*, published by Ikaros, 1965. Oil and pastel. *National Gallery, Alexandros Soutzos Museum, Athens. Photograph: Courtesy, the artist*

MEMORY, II (from LOGBOOK III)
George Seferis (1900–1971)

TRANSLATED BY EDMUND KEELEY AND PHILIP SHERRARD

EPHESUS

He spoke while sitting on what seemed to be
the marble remnant of an ancient gate;
endless the plain on the right and empty,
on the left the last shadows moved down the mountain:
"The poem is everywhere. Your voice
sometimes travels beside it
like a dolphin keeping company for a while
with a golden sloop in the sunlight,
then vanishing again. The poem is everywhere,
like the wings of the wind moved by the wind
to touch for a moment the sea gull's wings.
The same as our lives yet different too,
as a woman's face changes yet remains the same
after she strips naked. He who has loved
knows this; in the light that other people see things,
the world spoils; but you remember this:
Hades and Dionysus are the same."
He spoke and then took the main road
that leads to the old harbor, devoured now
under the rushes there. The twilight
as if ready for the death of some animal,
so naked was it.

           I remember still:
he was traveling to Ionian shores,
to empty shells of theaters
where only the lizard slithers over the dry stones,
and I asked him: "Will they be full again some day?"
and he answered: "Maybe, at the hour of death."
And he ran across the orchestra howling
"Let me hear my brother!"
And the silence surrounding us was harsh,
leaving no trace at all on the glass of the blue.

ON BOEOTIAN ROADS

Nikos Engonopoulos (1910–1985)

TRANSLATED BY KIMON FRIAR

beware: this swellfoot
we are about to encounter
on the forks of Boeotian roads
no: he is not the Oedipus of mythology

in spite of all the—so to speak—elephantism
of gout—the enlargement of extremities—
from which he suffers
this has no relation at all, I tell you, to the Oedipus of old

neither had he killed his father
nor—go, get there in time to tell Jocasta—
nor is he going to marry his mother

let him continue on ahead for a while
and then—in a little while again—he will vanish forever

but that black dog
that lies in the middle of the sun-washed road
"sun-washed" by the sun that is about to set
asleep or dead among the horse manure
eh! well, that one
that one is something

learn this: that one is the legendary Sphinx
who fell from her pedestal
when she saw
that "enigmas"
no longer exist

SPHINX.
7th century B.C.
Bronze.
Archaeological Museum, Olympia
Photograph: Courtesy Greek National Tourist Organization, Athens

WAITING FOR THE BARBARIANS
Constantine Cavafy (1863–1933)

TRANSLATED BY EDMUND KEELEY AND PHILIP SHERRARD

What are we waiting for, assembled in the forum?

> The barbarians are due here today.

Why isn't anything going on in the senate?
Why are the senators sitting there without legislating?

> Because the barbarians are coming today.
> What's the point of senators making laws now?
> Once the barbarians are here, they'll do the legislating.

Why did our emperor get up so early,
and why is he sitting enthroned at the city's main gate,
in state, wearing the crown?

> Because the barbarians are coming today
> and the emperor's waiting to receive their leader.
> He's even got a scroll to give him,
> loaded with titles, with imposing names.

Why have our two consuls and praetors come out today
wearing their embroidered, their scarlet togas?
Why have they put on bracelets with so many amethysts,
rings sparkling with magnificent emeralds?
Why are they carrying elegant canes
beautifully worked in silver and gold?

> Because the barbarians are coming today
> and things like that dazzle the barbarians.

Why don't our distinguished orators turn up as usual
to make their speeches, say what they have to say?

> Because the barbarians are coming today
> and they'd be bored by rhetoric and public speaking.

Why this sudden bewilderment, this confusion?
(How serious people's faces have become.)
Why are the streets and squares emptying so rapidly,
everyone going home lost in thought?

> Because night has fallen and the barbarians haven't come.
> And some of our men just in from the border say
> there are no barbarians any longer.

Now what's going to happen to us without barbarians?
Those people were a kind of solution.

Photograph of Constantine Cavafy.
1896.
Archives of Constantine Cavafy, Athens

Photograph of Angelos Sikelianos.
1920s.
Collection Anna Sikelianos, Athens

THE RETURN
Angelos Sikelianos (1884–1951)

TRANSLATED BY EDMUND KEELEY AND PHILIP SHERRARD

Holy, lion-like sleep
of the return, on the sand's
vast spaciousness.
In my heart my eyelids closed;
and radiance, like a sun, fills me.

The sea's sound floods my veins,
above me the sun
grinds like a millstone,
the wind beats its full wings;
the world's axle throbs heavily.
I cannot hear my deepest breath.
and the sea grows calm to the sand's edge
and spreads deep inside me.

The infinite caress exalts it
into a high-domed wave;
the cool seaweed
freshens me deep down;
the foam's lucid spindrift
breaks into spray on the pebbles;
beyond, where the cicadas stridulate,
the leaves' rustle dies away.

From far off comes a sound
and suddenly beats,
as a sail when the yard-arm breaks;
it is the wind approaching,
it is the sun setting before my eyes;
and in my purity I open my kindred eyelids
to its white presence.

I leap up. My lightness
is equal to my strength.
My cool forehead glows,
in the spring sunset
my body stirs profoundly,
I gaze around me: the Ionian sea,
and my delivered land!

THERMOPYLAE

Constantine Cavafy (1863–1933)

TRANSLATED BY EDMUND KEELEY AND PHILIP SHERRARD

Honor to those who in the life they lead
define and guard a Thermopylae.
Never betraying what is right,
consistent and just in all they do
but showing pity also, and compassion;
generous when they're rich, and when they're poor,
still generous in small ways,
still helping as much as they can;
always speaking the truth,
yet without hating those who lie.

And even more honor is due to them
when they foresee (as many do foresee)
that Ephialtes will turn up in the end,
that the Medes will break through after all.

YOUNG WARRIOR from the Sanctuary of Athena at Sounion.
460–360 B.C.
Marble.
National Archaeological Museum, Athens.
Photograph: TAP Service, Athens

Thracian women dancing.
1961.
Photograph: Constantine Manos / Magnum

TEMPTATION (from THE FREE BESEIGED)
Dionysios Solomos (1798–1857)

TRANSLATED BY RAE DALVEN

Love dances with yellow-haired April;
it is nature's good, sweet season,
and in the swelling shadows enfolding dew and musk
are languorous bird songs yet unheard.
Clear, sweet, graceful waters
pour into the musk-scented abyss,
taking its musk and leaving its freshness,
all revealing the wealth of their source to the sun,
darting here, there, like nightingales.
So too life gushes forth on earth, and sky and wave.
But on the waters of the lake, white and still,
still as far as the eye can see and clear to the depths,
the butterfly which makes its fragrant bed within the heart
of the wild lily, sports with its small strange shadow.
"Lovely dreamer, tell me what you have seen this night?"
"A night full of wonder, a night sown with magic!
No movement on earth or skies or seas,
not even as much as the bee makes near the tiny flower.
Around something motionless, whitening in the lake,
only the full moon moved
and a graceful girl rises clothed in its light."

ECLAT by Lynda Benglis.
1990.
Aluminum on stainless steel mesh.
Courtesy Paula Cooper Gallery, New York.
Photograph: Geoffrey Clements

REHEARSING FOR DEATH
Angelos Sikelianos (1884–1951)

TRANSLATED BY EDMUND KEELEY AND PHILIP SHERRARD

Memory has no end here and no beginning . . .

And there, from my being's depths, from the depths
where a god lay hidden in my mind's shadow,
the holy delirium was now set free,
and from the obscurity of my silences
powerful verses suddenly engulfed
my brain, quick verses, and they spoke these words:

'For You this bed is not a sick man's bed
but the secret trireme of Dionysus
that flies above the waves of time, above
the closed Rhythms of Creation, flies swiftly,
like an arrow, flies with great force.

Listen to Your freedom's sound; if all of You
was burning with fever but a while ago
and if Your body flamed like pine kindling,
it was so that You could find out how to burn.
Because now You are coming near the fire
that is not in creation but in the mind
of the Creator Himself. The star that shines
beside You is Hebe's, eternal Hebe's,
the star that pierces through the light of day.

You are no longer with what the sun illumines
but in Your depths You seem the burning life
of the sun's soul, You seem inside the sun,
and the flames that light the other stars, that light
the world, are now outside, outside of You.
You see the stars; the stars do not see You.
You see the world; the world does not see You.

You seem all hidden in Your passion's sun
and from there You aim Your arrows where
creation's stubbornness has not yet dawned.
For You this passion is a rehearsal for death:
rehearse it as is worthy of the holy fire
deep inside You, that Your mind encloses
not as created but as Creator.'

154

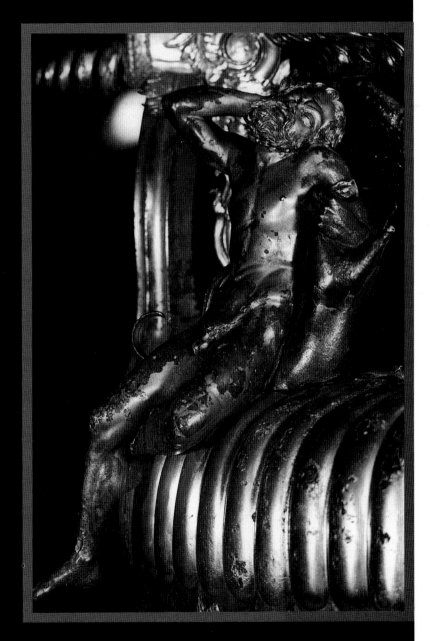

DERVENI KYLIX (detail of a satyr).
c. 330 B.C.
Bronze.
Archaeological Museum, Thessaloniki.
Photograph: Courtesy Greek National Tourist Organization, Athens

FROM LIFE IMMOVABLE
Costis Palamas (1859–1943)
TRANSLATED BY PHILIP SHERRARD

. . . . "—In the sun-glad nakedness
Of the Athenian day
If you should imagine
Something beastlike unclothed,
Something like a leafless
No shade conferring tree,
An unchiselled marble,
A body, slender, lean,

Something bare, uncovered,
In the open space
Which but two eyes of flame
Show to be alive;
Something which from the satyrs
Descends, and is wild,
And its voice is silver,
Do not flee: it is I,

The Satyr. Like the olive-tree
I am rooted here,
And with my pipe's refrain
I make the breezes faint.
I play and see! there mate,
Worship and are worshipped,
I play and see! there dance
Man, element, beast."

FROM "THRUSH" (III)
George Seferis (1900–1971)
TRANSLATED BY EDMUND KEELEY AND PHILIP SHERRARD

THE WRECK "THRUSH"

. . . . Light, angelic and black,
laughter of waves on the sea's highways,
tear-stained laughter,
the old suppliant sees you
as he moves to cross the invisible fields—
light mirrored in his blood,
the blood that gave birth to Eteocles and Polynices.
Day, angelic and black;
the brackish taste of woman that poisons the prisoner
emerges from the wave a cool branch adorned with drops.
Sing little Antigone, sing, O sing . . .
I'm not speaking to you about things past, I'm speaking
    about love;
decorate your hair with the sun's thorns,
dark girl;
the heart of the Scorpion has set,
the tyrant in man has fled,

and all the daughters of the sea, Nereids, Graeae,
hurry toward the shimmering of the rising goddess:
whoever has never loved will love,
in the light:

                      and you find yourself
in a large house with many windows open
running from room to room, not knowing from where to
    look out first,
because the pine-trees will vanish, and the mirrored moun-
    tains, and the chirping of birds
the sea will drain dry, shattered glass, from north and south
your eyes will empty of daylight
the way the cicadas suddenly, all together, fall silent.

THE DANCING HORAE from the Theater of Dionysos,
 Athens. 1st century, B.C.
Bas-relief, marble.
National Archaeological Museum, Athens.
Photograph: TAP Service, Athens

Illustration by Yannis Moralis for the poem "Axion Esti"
by Odysseus Elytis. 1959.
Lithograph.
Collection the artist

FROM AXION ESTI
Odysseus Elytis (Born 1911)

TRANSLATED BY EDMUND KEELEY AND GEORGE SAVIDIS

Intelligible sun of Justice and you, glorifying myrtle,
do not, I implore you, do not forget my country!

Its high mountains eagle-shaped, its volcanos all vines in rows,
and its houses the whiter for neighboring near the blue!

Though touching Asia on one side and Europe a little on the other,
it stands there alone in the air and alone in the sea!

Neither a foreigner's concept nor a kinsman's one love,
but mourning, oh, everywhere and the relentless light!

My bitter hands circle with the Thunderbolt to the other side of Time,
I summon my old friends with threats and running blood!

But the blood has all been ransomed and, oh, the threats quarried,
and the winds rush in now, the one against the other!

Intelligible sun of Justice and you, glorifying myrtle,
do not, I implore you, do not forget my country!

Man holding a staff.
1930s.
Benaki Museum, Athens. Photographic Archive
Photograph: Nelly's

158

THE POET (FROM LITURGY UNDER THE ACROPOLIS)
Nikiphoros Vrettakos (1912–1991)

TRANSLATED BY MARIOS BYRON RAIZIS

I, about to retire, profoundly happy, honored to be of your earth, was not "sent from heaven to say hail."
I ascended from your innards and I return to your innards.
Light from your light and sadness from your sadness flow in my wrinkles.
I do not know whether with what I have said I have paid off my debt to your hospitality.
Nor if through the sun I have responded to the sun your spirit.

Because it is here that I breathed your air and my whole body glowed.
I heard inside me my soul conversing with you and I discovered it.
Because it is here that, drinking your water, I made it eternally good to drink.
And here that the sun directed an ever-flowing shaft of rays in my heart, and their two centres were joined for good.
And from here they were thrust into my whole body opening new veins where Genesis had not foreseen any.
In my hair and bones.
And my whole soul was washed in the sun.

And I drank from your vineyard that climbs to heaven, and spreads itself in the light over the sea.
And when I brought to my mouth grapes, mulberries, or peaches, I felt as if you were giving me suckle.

And your unuttered word taught me everything.
My heart and sight were filled with wisdom.

So that, when I said "sun" or "light" or "God," I knew what I was talking about.
Because you placed within me the holy gift of love, made of flowers of truth.
And it is with those that I have woven your little wreath today that resembles a small sun circle.

And now, look: with the very hand that wrote hymns to the light, I take some earth from your earth.
I kiss you and wish you "Eternal Life, Eternal Light, Eternal Logos": your thrice-thousand-millionth little son.

THE CARYATIDS
Andreas Embiricos (1901–1975)

TRANSLATED BY KIMON FRIAR

O the breasts of youth
O the pallid waters of the fig-peckers
The pavements resound with the steps of the morning people
O vigorous groves with your trees of crimson
Youth knows of your meaning
Already dawning upon your fringes
Tassels of eiderdown frisk among the breasts of young girls
Who walk half-naked in your little bypaths
Their hair is more beautiful than that of Absalom
Among the locks the drops of amber fall
And the dark-skinned girls come carrying leaves of ebony
The squirrels sniff at their footprints
The woods are deeply moved
The woods are swarming with legions of brandishing lances
Here even the larks strip themselves of their shadows
The streetcars cannot be heard
And the day is sighing
For one of her very small daughters is fondling the day's nipples
And a spanking will do no good
Only a deer goes by holding in his mouth
The three cherries he had found between the breasts of youth
The evenings here are warm
The trees enwrap themselves in their silence
Rocks of silence drop now and then into the clearing
As the light does before it breaks into day.

UNTITLED by Robert Rauschenberg.
1985.
Acrylic and collage on fabric laminated paper mounted on canvas.
Marx Collection, Berlin.
Photograph: Courtesy the artist

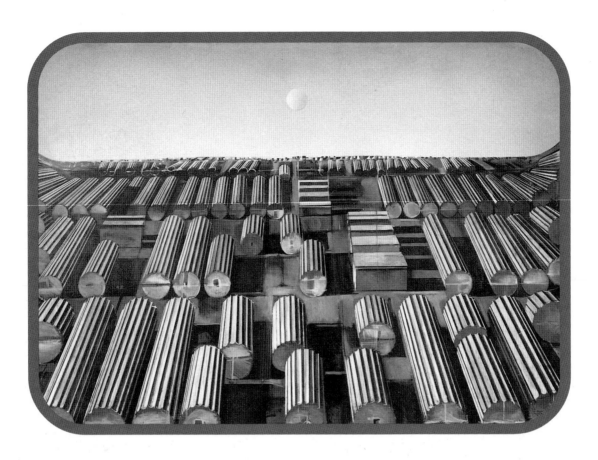

GREEK LANDSCAPE
by Dimitris Mytaras.
1972.
Oil on canvas.
Private collection

COLUMNS OF THE TEMPLE OF OLYMPIAN ZEUS
Nicolas Calas (1907–1988)

TRANSLATED BY KIMON FRIAR

At night the azure columns of the temple turn pale
but lift their wounded stature to unreachable skies in vain
no one understands the wordless supplication of an old adoration
directed to Zeus by the suggestive lines of chiseled stone
the acanthi have rusted and the fearless capitals are blown bodily
by erotic winds that seek refuge there
these marbles have been reduced to being liturgists of the hymen
any other meaning they had has vanished
archeologists strive in vain to find a coherence
in fragments that history has cast far away from itself
the muted members lie on the ground
not even one footfall of a faithful follower disturbs them
not a single shadow reechoes amid the ruins
and these have betrayed my walk
its purpose has vanished in a night far distant from its starless roof
and the coherence of history has vanished, cannot be found.

I become envious of these cold stone masses
that have been standing here wordless for centuries now
listening to the sweet echo of past emotions.

Fragments of statues and leaves.
Photograph: Courtesy Greek National Tourist Organization, Athens

RETURN
Yannis Ritsos (1909–1991)
TRANSLATED BY EDMUND KEELEY

The statues left first. A little later
the trees, people, animals. The land
became entirely desert. The wind blew.
Newspapers and thorns circled in the streets.
At dusk the lights went on by themselves.
A man came back alone, looked around him,
took out his key, stuck it in the ground
as though entrusting it to an underground hand
or as though planting a tree. Then he climbed
the marble stairs and gazed down at the city.
Cautiously, one by one, the statues returned.

DELPHI CHARIOTEER, detail of the head. c. 477 B.C. Bronze.
Archaeological Museum, Delphi. Photograph: David Finn, New York

THE CHARIOTEER OF DELPHI
James Merrill (Born 1926)

Where are the horses of the sun?

Their master's green bronze hand, empty of all
But a tangle of reins, seems less to call
His horses back than to wait out their run.

To cool that havoc and restore
The temperance we had loved them for
I have implored him, child, at your behest.

Watch now, the flutings of his dress hang down
From the brave patina of breast.
His gentle eyes glass brown

Neither attend us nor the latest one
Blistered and stammering who comes to cry
Village in flames and river dry,

None to control the chariot
And to call back the killing horses none
Now that their master, eyes ashine, will not.

For watch, his eyes in the still air alone
Look shining and nowhere
Unless indeed into our own

Who are reflected there
Littler than dolls wound up by a child's fear
How tight, their postures only know.

And loosely, watch now, the reins overflow
His fist, as if once more the unsubdued
Beasts shivering and docile stood

Like us before him. Do you remember how
A small brown pony would
Nuzzle the cube of sugar from your hand?

Broken from his mild reprimand
In fire and fury hard upon the taste
Of a sweet license, even these have raced

Uncurbed in us, where fires are fanned.

DELPHI CHARIOTEER. c. 477 B.C. Bronze.
Archaeological Museum, Delphi. Photograph: David Finn, New York

AESCHYLUS (525–456 B.C.). Born in Athens, he died in Gela, Sicily. He wrote more than seventy plays of which seven have survived—*The Persians, The Seven Against Thebes, Oresteia (Agamemnon, The Libation Bearers, The Eumenides), The Suppliants,* and *Prometheus.* He is a major poet in the world of Greek tragedy.

ALCAEUS (c. 600 B.C.). A contemporary of Sappho, who was also born on the island of Lesbos, Alcaeus wrote in the local Aeolic dialect. Although a member of the nobility, he attacked the ruling parties in his poetry. He uses myth and metaphor, but he also celebrates the pleasures of everyday life.

ANACREON (563–478 B.C.). He was born in Teos, in Asia Minor, then he lived in Samos and in Athens. The elegance and charm of his poetry were always greatly admired. There are approximately sixty lyric poems, which were composed by various authors in imitation of Anacreon's style during a period from 500 B.C. to 200 B.C.

ARCHILOCHUS (c. 750–650 B.C.). A Greek poet from the island of Paros, regarded as the first of the lyric poets and ranked by the ancients with Homer and Pindar. Even Plato calls him "the very wise." Only fragments of his work are extant.

ARISTOPHANES (450–385 B.C.). Born in Athens, friend of Socrates, twice prosecuted for his outspoken political attacks, Aristophanes wrote forty plays of which several have survived. Among them are: *Wasps, The Frogs, Lysistrata, Clouds, Acharnians, Thesmophoriazusae, Ecclesiazusae,* and *The Birds.*

BACCHYLIDES (505–450 B.C.). A lyric poet from Ceos, and nephew of Simonides. He wrote dithyrambs, odes, hymns, and paeans. His reputation has suffered by comparison with Pindar, although his gifts are of a different kind: a brilliant clarity and sense of narrative, a real love for the games which he describes, a choice command of epithets, and occasional moments of magical beauty.

BORGES, JORGE LUIS (1899–1986). An Argentinian writer, born in Buenos Aires, he was educated there and at Geneva and Cambridge. His stories, which he called *Ficciones,* exerted a fascination that translation in no way diminished, since they presented weirdly erudite crumbs from a bibliophile's banquet. He worked as a prominent librarian and director of the Buenos Aires National Library.

BYRON, GEORGE GORDON (1788–1824). Born in London, he traveled extensively in southern Europe and the Levant. Among his works: *Childe Harold, The Dream, Don Juan.* He exerted a great influence on the Romantic movement. In 1823 Byron went to Greece and joined the Greek insurgents. He died of fever at Missolonghi in April 1824.

CALAS, NICOLAS (1907–1988). Born in Lausanne, he was brought up in Athens and died in New York. Increasingly concerned with aesthetic matters from a surrealist point of view, he first published poetry and later a series of essays on art's relation to aesthetics and culture. He also taught at Fairleigh Dickinson University, New Jersey, where he was Professor of Art. *Art in the Age of Risk* is a collection of his articles on art.

CAVAFY, CONSTANTINE (1863–1933). Born in Alexandria, Egypt, he spent most of his life there. His poems use words from Ancient, Byzantine, and Medieval Greece, often in a Hellenistic setting. They are dramatic and often ironic. In English translation: *The Poems of C. P. Cavafy,* translated by John Mavrogordato; *The Complete Poems of C. P. Cavafy,* translated by Rae Dalven; *C. P. Cavafy Collected Poems,* translated by Edmund Keeley and Philip Sherrard.

CORNAROS, VIZENTZOS (16th–17th century). The most significant poet of the Cretan Renaissance. In his poem *Erotocritos* (probably written between 1646 and 1669), he recounts the love of Erotocritos and Aretousa in ten thousand "political" couplets. The *Erotocritos* has been translated into English in its entirety.

DURRELL, LAWRENCE GEORGE (1912–1990). English novelist, poet, travel writer, and playwright, he was born in India. He took numerous odd jobs and traveled widely as a journalist. His reputation was greatly enhanced by the *Alexandria Quartet,* a complex interlocking series of four books set in Egypt, remarkable for its sensuous language, intrigue and devious plotting—the nature of modern love being its central topic.

ELYTIS, ODYSSEUS (Born 1911). A native of Herakleion, Crete, he lives in Athens. He studied in France and won the Nobel Prize for Poetry in 1979. He is the poet of the sun and the sea with a great plastic use of language and imagery. In English: *The Sovereign Sun, Axion Esti, Maria Nephele, Selected Poems, Analogies of Light.*

EMBIRICOS, ANDREAS (1901–1975). Born on the island Andros, he lived in Paris where he became a member of the surrealistic group headed by Andre Breton. He is the first Greek surrealist poet. In English translation: *Amour Amour, Writing on Personal Mythology,* and poems in various anthologies.

ENGONOPOULOS, NIKOS (1910–1985). He was the foremost Greek surrealist painter. He participated in the Biennale in Venice in 1954, and was Professor of Art in the School of Architecture in Athens. Simultaneously, he was a very well-known surrealist poet.

EURIPIDES (480–406 B.C.). Born in Athens, he left later for the Court of King Archelaus of Macedonia. Of his eighty-eight plays, only nineteen have survived. Among them are: *Alcestis, Medea, The Heracleidae, Hippolytus, Iphigeneia in Tauris, Helen, The Trojan Women, Ion, The Suppliant Women,* and *The Bacchae.*

FOSCOLO, UGO (1778–1827). Born in Zakynthos, he was of Greek and Venetian descent. He was the first of the triad of early nineteenth-century writers—Foscolo, Manzoni, Leopardi—who gave the Italians works of outstanding creative originality during their laborious quest for nationhood. His best poem, *I Sepolcri,* was published in 1807. He also wrote two tragedies and published various works in London, where he sought refuge after 1814.

GATSOS, NICOS (1911–1992). Born in the Peloponnesus, he has written many lyrics for the well-known Greek composers. He is primarily the author of *Amorgos,* which has had a strong influence on the writers of his generation.

GRAVES, ROBERT (1895–1986). English poet, novelist, essayist and critic, he was born in London. His best poetry, written between about 1928 and 1943, is lucid, tender, and evocative. He also wrote such historical novels as *I, Claudius* and *Claudius the God. The White Goddess* is his most significant non-fiction title, its credo being that real poets receive their gifts from the Muse. His fascination with myth is apparent in his *Greek Myths* and *Hebrew Myths.*

HOMER (? 9th century B.C.). The great Greek epic poet to whom tradition attributes two distinct but complementary epics: the *Iliad* (telling of the Trojan war) and the *Odyssey* (telling of the wandering of Odysseus on his way back to Ithaca). Nothing is known about Homer with certainty, but according to tradition, he lived in Ionia (four city-states claimed to have been his birthplace). Homer's lifetime seems to have coincided with the introduction of writing into the Greek world and he may have utilized the new technique by committing his verses to writing, or dictating them to others.

HESIOD (c. 800 B.C.). He lived in Boeotia, and was the author of *Theogony,* a dramatic and primitive version of the origins of the world, and *Works and Days* about everyday life.

HÖLDERLIN, JOHANN CHRISTIAN FRIEDRICH (1770–1843). A German poet, he was born in Lauffen. He studied theology at Tübingen and philosophy with Schelling and Hegel. His early poetry owes much to Schiller and to Susette Gontard, the "Diotima" of his works, whose inspiration helped him to discover his true poetical self. He wrote, among others, the philosophical novel *Hyperion* (1799) and the magnificent elegy *Menon's Lament for Diotima,* which examines the discrepancy between the actually and the ideally possible.

IBYKOS (c. 560 B.C.). He was born at Rhegium in Italy, but he left for the court of Polykrates, the ruler of Samos. He wrote narrative poetry. His erotic poetry resembles the lyricism of Sappho.

KALVOS, ANDREAS (1792–1869). Born in Zakynthos, he traveled and lived most of his life in Europe, where he became a friend of Ugo Foscolo. It was among the Philhellenes in Italy that he tried to coordinate a revival of ancient Greek culture.

KAROUZOS, NIKOS (1926–1990). Born in Nafplion, he produced a deeply existential and metaphysical type of poetry. With a lyric accuracy he suggested, sometimes epigrammatically, that love is the only remedy for the personal anguish and the absurdity of our times. Some of his poetical works (*Lindos, Poems, Terrifying Joy*) have appeared in English-language translations in various literary journals.

KAZANTZAKIS, NIKOS (1883–1957). Born in Herakleion, Crete, he died in Germany. He traveled in many parts of the world and wrote many travel books. He translated Homer, Dante, and Goethe and wrote his own long epic, *The Odyssey: A Modern Sequel* (translated into English). He wrote many novels, plays, and film scripts, an autobiography, philosophical studies and essays, and was nominated several times for the Nobel Prize. Some of his books available in English are: *Zorba the Greek, The Greek Passion, The Last Temptation of Christ, Saint Francis,* and *Freedom or Death.*

KEATS, JOHN (1795–1821). Born in London, he was a friend of Shelley. He composed the odes: *On A Grecian Urn, To A Nightingale, To Autumn, On Melancholy, On Indolence, To Psyche.* He died in Rome. On his tomb he asked that these words be engraved: "Here lies one whose name was writ in water."

LAWRENCE, DAVID HERBERT (1885–1930). A novelist, he lived mostly abroad in Italy, Australia, and New Mexico. Among his best known novels are: *The White Peacock, Sons and Lovers, Women in Love,* and *Lady Chatterley's Lover.* He also published several volumes of poems.

MAVILIS, LORENZO (1860–1912). He was from the Ionian Islands. He translated works from many foreign languages, including Sanskrit, and was well known for his sonnets, as well as his patriotism.

MELEAGER (c. 90 B.C.). Born in Gadara, he spent his adult life on the island of Kos. He wrote more than 130 epigrams, which were mostly about love. His collection of epigrams, the so-called "Garland of Meleager," was one of the first attempts to create an anthology of Greek poetry.

MERRILL, JAMES (Born 1926). He is the author of eleven books of poems, which have won him two National Book Awards (for *Nights and Days* and *Mirabell*), the Bollingen Prize in Poetry (for *Braving the Elements*), and the Pulitzer Prize (for *Divine Comedies*)—as well as novels, plays, and essays.

MILTON, JOHN (1608–1674). He was educated at Cambridge University, England and became well-known for the poem *On The Morning of Christ's Nativity* (1629). His most famous works are *Paradise Lost* (started in 1642 and finished in 1667), and *Paradise Regained* (which he wrote while blind and finished in 1671). In 1643 he published a pamphlet on *The Doctrine and Discipline of Divorce* and later the *Areopagitica*, which was inspired by ancient Greek democracy.

MIMNERMUS (c. 630 B.C.). He is mainly considered a love poet obsessed by the ephemeral quality of youth and the horror of old age. His work exists only in fragments, which have been conveyed to us by other writers.

OVID (PUBLIUS OVIDIUS NASO) (43 B.C.–A.D. 17). A Roman poet, born in Sulmo. He was trained for the law in Rome but devoted himself to poetry. His literary successes include his tragedy *Medea*, as well as his *Epistulae* and *Heroides*, imaginary love letters from women of the heroic days to their lovers, and his *Amores*, short poems about his mistress Corinna. His true masterpieces are the *Ars Amatoria* and the epic *Metamorphoses* in fifteen books. For some unknown reason he was banished to Tomi on the Black Sea, where he died.

PALAMAS, COSTIS (1859–1943). Born in Patras, Greece, he was the leader of the so-called "generation of the eighties" (1880s). His poetry reflects a turn in Modern Greek history, when the bourgeois structure prevailed in society. He wrote entirely in the demotic language, trying to reconcile folk tradition with erudite poetry. He managed to join the Greek national tradition and Western thought, using meters and rhythms which paved the way for the Modern Greek poetry of our century. Some of his most important poetic compositions, translated into English are: *Iambs and Anapaests* (1897), *Life Immovable* (1904), *The Twelve Words of the Gypsy* (1907), and *The King's Flute* (1910).

PAPAIOANNOU, YANNIS (1913–1972). A musician and lyricist who wrote hundreds of songs, he was known for his *rebetika*—the music that began in the jails of Greek towns and became the popular bouzouki music of the 1930s, 1940s, and 1950s. It has many parallels with American blues—like the blues, the *rebetika* songs were the soul music of a group of people who felt themselves to be outside the mainstream of society and who developed their own forms of expression.

PAUL THE SILENTIARY (c. A.D. 563). Silentiarius ("private secretary") was a high official at Justinian's court. Some eighty of his epigrams, vivid aesthetic fancies inspired by pictures, are in the *Greek Anthology*. He also wrote an elaborate *ekphrasis* of the restored church of St. Sophia.

PHERAIOS, RHIGAS (1759–1798). Born in Thessaly, he struggled through his political and ethnic actions to prepare the ground for the Greek revolution against the Ottomans. He published several books, as well as the *Big Chart of the Freed Greece* in Vienna. His *War Song* circulated secretly in pamphlets and—with its visionary enthusiasm—encouraged the Greeks to revolt and fight for their freedom.

PINDAR (c. 438 B.C.). He was born in Boeotia to an aristocratic family who sent him to study music and poetry in Athens. He was commissioned by the royal House of Thessaly at the age of twenty to write the ode *Pythian X*. He became very famous for his Epinician Odes (choral songs), which were written in honor of victories in the great Games.

RITSOS, YANNIS (1909–1991). Author of seventy-seven volumes of poetry as well as plays, essays, and translations, his work has been translated into forty-four languages and he has been honored with numerous awards worldwide. Tyranny, oppression, torture, and degradation are reflected in the nightmarish imagery of his poetry, but there are also lyrical and idyllic interludes, together with clever recreations of Greek mythology and history. In English translation: *Gestures and Other Poems, Selected Poems, Eighteen Short Songs for the Bitter Motherland, Chronicle of Exile, The Fourth Dimension, The Moonlight Sonata,* and *Repetitions, Testimonies, Parentheses.*

SAPPHO (c. 600 B.C.). Born on the isle of Lesbos to an aristocratic family, she was an unparalleled lyricist and one of the most famous and influential of all Greek poets. It is believed that she was the head of a sisterhood dedicated to the veneration of Aphrodite. Many of her poems—of which we have only fragments—were written in celebration of the marriages of young girls.

SEFERIS, GEORGE (1900–1971). Born in Smyrna, Asia Minor, he died in Athens. He was educated in France and served as a diplomat in many countries. He was the first Greek poet to be awarded the Nobel Prize in Literature in 1963. His poetry transcends the particular and ephemeral, and attains the universal and permanent. In the tragic fate of Hellenism and of his generation, Seferis grasped the universal anguish of our times. His poetry has been extensively translated into English: *Collected Poems,* as well as his *Essays on Poetry and Hellenism,* and parts of his *Journal: Days of 1945–1951.*

SHELLEY, PERCY BYSSHE (1792–1822). He was educated at Oxford and spent many years in Italy, where he became a friend of Lord Byron. Some of his best-known works are: *Hymn to Intellectual Beauty,* Odes *To Naples* and *To Liberty,* the notable *Defense of Poetry,* the great lyrical dramas *Prometheus Unbound,* and *Hellas* (inspired by the struggle of Greece for freedom). He drowned at the age of thirty while writing the *Triumph of Life.*

SIKELIANOS, ANGELOS (1884–1951). The focus of his life was the formation of Delphic festivals in Delphi in 1927 and 1930. He has been nominated for the Nobel Prize in Poetry. He is a poet of high visions and wide rhetorical wit—his work is full of lyricism and poetic drama. In English translation: *Six Poems From The Greek, Sikelianos and Seferis, Akriton Songs, Selected Poems.*

SOLOMOS, DIONYSIOS (1798–1857). Born in Zakynthos, he was educated in Italy where he began writing poetry in Italian. He then returned to Corfu where he wrote in demotic Greek. In 1823 he wrote the *Hymn to Liberty* from which the first quatrains were taken for the Greek national anthem. His main works available in English translations are: *The Free Besieged, Porphyras, The Cretans.* Together with Andreas Kalvos, he is a primary figure in the School of the Ionian Islands.

SOPHOCLES (496–406 B.C.). Born in Athens, he was a friend of Pericles and Herodotus. He wrote over 100 plays for the Athenian theater but only seven of them survive—*Antigone, Oedipus the King, Oedipus at Colonus, Electra, Ajax, The Trachinian Maidens,* and *Philoctetes.* He is supposed to have said that he showed men as they ought to be, and that Euripides showed them as they actually were.

TSATSOS, IOANNA (Born 1919). Born in Smyrna, Asia Minor, sister of Nobel Laureate George Seferis, and wife to Academician Constantine Tsatsos. An ardent humanist, she studied law and was involved for decades in social, political, and cultural activities. Some of the central themes in her poetry, which she treats with intuition and sensitivity, are the concepts of love, religious faith, the passage of time, and death. A selection of her poetry has been translated into English (*Poems,* 1984), as well as into French.

VIGNY, ALFRED VICTOR, COMTE DE (1797–1863). A French Romantic writer who served in the Royal Guards, he failed in his attempt to enter Parliament, and had an unhappy domestic life. This is reflected in his work, especially in that masterpiece of Romantic drama, *Chatterton* (1835). Other notable works include the play *Othello* (1829), and the philosophical poems *Les Destinées* (1864), all exemplifying Vigny's pessimism.

VRETTAKOS, NIKIPHOROS (1912–1991). Prolific poet who hated injustice and believed that art must be the expression of love, peace, and goodness. He produced poetry of a highly ideological nature, reflecting his Christian and humanistic ideals. Some of his poems (*Fever, Dialogue with Poetry, Liturgy under the Acropolis,* etc.) have been translated into English in numerous literary journals.

WILDE, OSCAR (1856–1900). Irish poet, born in Dublin, educated there and at Oxford. He became a leader in the aesthetic movement with its principle of art for art's sake, and his flamboyant lifestyle made him one of the most famous men of his time. As a result of his friendship with Lord Alfred Douglas, he was sentenced to two years imprisonment for homosexuality. After his release he wrote *The Ballad of Reading Gaol* (1898). Wilde's poetry disappeared from the stage and his books were ostracized after his conviction, but his literary reputation was gradually restored in the new century. Among his works: *The Happy Prince* (fairy tales, 1888) and *The Picture of Dorian Grey* (1891).

YEATS, WILLIAM BUTLER (1865–1939). Irish poet, born in Dublin. His interest in the indigenous Irish tradition contributed to the leading part he played in the Celtic revival and the Irish literary rebirth. His early poetry is mystical and romantic, and he became famous for *Poems* (1895), *The Wind among the Reeds* (1899), and *In the Seven Woods* (1903), among other volumes. In 1922 he was made a senator of the Irish Free State, and in 1923 he was awarded the Nobel Prize. He also helped to found the Abbey Theatre, encouraging the work of John M. Synge and Sean O'Casey, among others.

ACKNOWLEDGMENTS

Grateful acknowledgment is made for permission to reproduce the poems and illustrations in this book. All possible care has been taken to trace ownership of every selection and to make full acknowledgment (for illustrations, sources are included in accompanying captions). If any errors or omissions have occurred, they will be corrected in subsequent editions, provided that notification is sent to the publisher.

POETRY

"About 'Peace'" from "Paean" in *Bacchylides: Complete Poems*, translated by Robert Fagles. © Copyright 1961 by Robert Fagles. Reprinted by permission of Yale University Press. "Achilles and Priam." From *The Iliad* by Homer. Translated by Robert Fagles. Translation copyright © 1990 by Robert Fagles. Introduction and notes copyright © Bernard Knox, 1990. Used by permission of Viking Penguin, a division of Penguin Books USA Inc. and Georges Borchardt Inc. From "Agamemnon" in *The Oresteia* by Aeschylus. Translated by Robert Fagles. Translation copyright © 1966, 1967, 1975 by Robert Fagles. Used by permission of Viking Penguin, a division of Penguin Books USA Inc. and Georges Borchardt Inc. "Akathistos Hymn." Translated by Constantine A. Trypanis, from *The Penguin Book of Greek Verse*, edited by Constantine A. Trypanis (Penguin Books, 1971), copyright © Constantine A. Trypanis, 1971. All rights reserved. Reproduced by permission of Penguin Books Ltd. "Alkinoos Garden" from *The Odyssey* by Homer, translated by R. Fitzgerald. Copyright © 1961, 1963 by Robert Fitzgerald and renewed 1989 by Benedict R.C. Fitzgerald. Reprinted by permission of Vintage Books, a Division of Random House, Inc. "The Alphabet of Love." From *The Charioteer*, No. 5 (1963): pp. 68–72. Translated by Theodore Stephanidis. Copyright © Pella Publishing Co. Inc. Reprinted by permission. "The Altar of the Fatherland" by Andreas Kalvos, translated by Philip Sherrard in *The Wound Of Greece, Studies in Neo-Hellenism* by Philip Sherrard (Rex Collins, London, and Denise Harvey, Athens, 1978). Books for Libraries Press, Freeport, NY. Copyright 1956 by Vallentine, Mitchell & Co. Ltd. Reprinted 1970 by arrangement. "Amorgos" by Nicos Gatsos from *Voices of Modern Greece, Cavafy, Sikelianos, Seferis, Elytis, and Gatsos*. Lockert Library of Poetry in Translation, copyright © 1981 by Princeton University Press. Used with permission, pp. 180–181. From "Anniversary" by Odysseus Elytis. From *Odysseus Elytis: Selected Poems*, chosen and introduced by Edmund Keeley and Philip Sherrard. Translation copyright © 1981 by Edmund Keeley and Philip Sherrard. Used by permission of Viking Penguin, a division of Penguin Books USA Inc. and by Anvil Press Poetry, London. From "Antigone" by Sophocles. From *Three Theban Plays*, translated by Robert Fagles. Translation copyright © 1982 by Robert Fagles. Used by permission of Viking Penguin, a division of Penguin Books USA Inc. and Georges Borchardt Inc. "The Argonauts" from *The Complete Poems of D. H. Lawrence* by D. H. Lawrence. Copyright © 1964, 1971 by Angelo Ravagli and C. M. Weekley, Executors of the Estate of Frieda Lawrence Ravagli. Used by permission of Viking Penguin, a division of Penguin Books USA Inc. and Laurence Pollinger Ltd. "As much as you can" from *C.P. Cavafy: Collected Poems*, translated by Edmund Keeley and Philip Sherrard, ed. George Savidis. Trans. copyright © 1975 by Edmund Kee-

INDEX OF POEMS

INDEX OF POETS

INDEX OF ILLUSTRATIONS